GE
HOU
Handbook

A DAVID & CHARLES BOOK
Copyright © David & Charles Limited 2008

David & Charles is an F+W Publications Inc. company
4700 East Galbraith Road
Cincinnati, OH 45236

First published in 1997 as *Georgian House Style*
This revised edition first published in 2008

Original edition first published in 1997 as *Georgian House Style*, conceived and designed by John Strange and Megra Mitchell.

Copyright © Megra Mitchell 1997, 2001–2008

Text copyright © Ingrid Cranfield 1997, 2001–2008

Ingrid Cranfield has asserted her right to be identified as author of this work in accordance with the Copyright, Designs and Patents Act, 1988.

A catalogue record for this book is available from the British Library.

ISBN-13: 978-0-7153-2873-6 paperback
ISBN-10: 0-7153-2873-5 paperback

Printed in Singapore by KHL Printing Co Pte Ltd
for David & Charles
Brunel House, Newton Abbot, Devon

Commissioning Editor: Jane Trollope
Project Editor: James Loader
Editor: Emily Pitcher
Desk Editor: Demelza Hookway
Senior Designer: Sarah Clark
Page Layouts: Lorraine Inglis
Production Controller: Ros Napper

Visit our website at www.davidandcharles.co.uk

David & Charles books are available from all good bookshops; alternatively you can contact our Orderline on 0870 9908222 or write to us at FREEPOST EX2 110, D&C Direct, Newton Abbot, TQ12 4ZZ (no stamp required UK only); US customers call 800-289-0963 and Canadian customers call 800-840-5220.

GEORGIAN HOUSE STYLE
Handbook

INGRID CRANFIELD
EDITED BY JAMES LOADER

D&C
David and Charles

Contents

Introduction

'Materials in architecture are like words in Phraseology which singly have little or no power, and may be so arranged as to excite contempt yet when combined with Art, and expressed with energy, they actuate the mind with unbounded sway.'

William Chambers, 1798

The Georgian period is normally taken to refer to the reigns of George I (1714–27), his son George II (1727–60), his grandson George III (1760–1820) and George IV (1820–30). The period 1811–20, when George IV, then Prince of Wales, ruled as Regent on behalf of his insane father, is known as the Regency.

England was at peace between 1713 and 1739, but the eighteenth century as a whole was a period of war and diplomacy, marked by the emergence of a newly independent America. Towards the end of the century industrial output soared, while in the countryside, the enclosure of fields, mainly by acts of Parliament, brought more land under cultivation. Rural rents rose and so did farm profits, but many former small owner-occupiers became labourers or had to turn to other livelihoods: some ended as paupers.

All was not misery and hopelessness, however. The eighteenth century, according to some historians, witnessed the 'birth of the consumer society', and certainly fashion and taste became widespread preoccupations, filtering down from the élite at least as far as the provincial middle classes. Bath and Bristol and other spa towns boomed; romanticism blossomed in the arts; the Grand Tour through France, Italy and Germany became the desideratum of the well-to-do.

The Industrial Revolution in the eighteenth and early nineteenth centuries produced a great leap forward, with towns such as Manchester, Sheffield and York growing dramatically. The different towns had many features in common, in particular, working-class housing in long rows of brick terraces. The great demand for new houses now developed into a passion of construction. Landed gentry and aristocrats desired town houses in addition to, and often in the same style as, their country homes.

Previous page: Georgian homes would sometimes have a room designated as a 'print room', in which the walls were covered with engravings of ornate frames and pictures.

Above: A mid-eighteenth-century ceiling design.

Left: Chimneypiece bearing a relief depicting a sacrifice to Bacchus, carved by Michael Rysbrack, one of the foremost sculptors of the early eighteenth century; Clandon Park, Surrey.

Georgian house style was born in London out of a marriage between speculative wealth and taste, and a practical desire for permanence. In 1615, Inigo Jones's design for the Queen's House at Greenwich (now part of the National Maritime Museum) was one of the first great initiators of change.

The Duke of Bedford adopted this new style for the construction of the Covent Garden Piazza (now nearly all destroyed), where plain brick houses were built in terraces forming a central open space on the Italian pattern. In about 1640 a row of red-brick houses in Great Queen Street nearby was built and presumably designed in a free version of Jones's style by Peter Mills, a bricklayer, complete with tall and narrow casement windows and a Classical wooden cornice at eaves level. This scheme, with continuous terraces in two rows facing each other, constituted what was, in the eighteenth century, reputed to be 'the first regular street in London'.

It also set in place a canon of design for elevations. Here was the basis of the Classicism that characterized so much of Georgian building. House façades represented a Classical order in the form of a column raised on a podium, with the ground floor corresponding to the podium, the upper floors to the column, and the emphasis at first-floor level, from which the main part of the order arose. Palladianism – a return to the Classical canons of architectural design as laid down by Andrea Palladio (1508–80) and interpreted principally by Jones – became the norm of British architecture, not only at the highest levels in great public buildings but throughout the land, permeating the workshops of the most modest carpenter and bricklayer.

Right: The marble hall of Clandon Park, built in Classical style by the Venetian architect Giacomo Leoni c.1731, for the second Lord Onslow. The hall is a single 12.2m (40ft) cube, with two chimneypieces, each with a relief carved by Michael Rysbrack.

This time, too, witnessed the heyday of the speculative builder; with the growth in population and demand for housing in towns. Furthermore, it was soon realized that houses on their own could not provide a satisfactory living environment: they had to be part of a complete unit of development, comprising a square, some smaller, less expensive streets, a market and perhaps a church.

The Great Fire of London in 1660 shifted the course of building development. The Act for the Rebuilding of the City of London in 1667 was an extremely comprehensive measure, imposing the strictest regulations to ensure maximum fireproofing. Precise thicknesses of walls, which had to be of brick or stone, were also fixed, as were the sizes of timbers to be used for floors and roofs. Wood was banned from the outside of all houses except for beams over openings in the walls, which had to be of fire-resistant oak or, later, fir. The Act was enormously successful in promoting sound construction, partly because of its detailed provisions, and partly because it merely crystallized good practice and accentuated certain desirable trends. Its effect on the design of the individual house was so profound that similar patterns appeared in other parts of the country and, in due course, in the colonies.

Georgian house style was influenced as much by advances in technology as by changes in the law. The Industrial Revolution brought new materials and techniques in sources of fuel, types of brick, plasterwork, iron and glass technology, paint, plumbing and drainage systems and lighting methods, among others. These practical developments tied in with and facilitated the realization of the ideals, or sometimes mere whims, of those who introduced, determined and promulgated new styles and tastes.

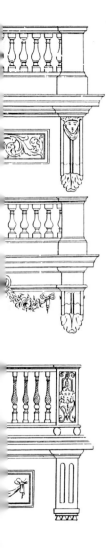

Below: Drawing by Thomas H. Shepherd of Sussex Place, Regent's Park, London, published 5 May 1827. This was one of a series of 'views of the new and most interesting objects in the British metropolis & its vicinity'.

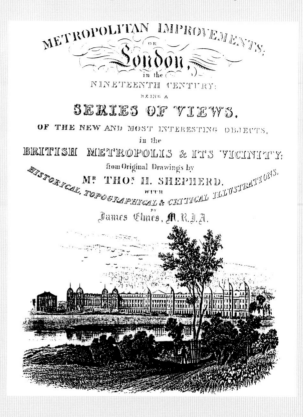

METROPOLITAN IMPROVEMENTS;
OR
London,
in the
NINETEENTH CENTURY:
BEING A
SERIES OF VIEWS,
OF THE NEW AND MOST INTERESTING OBJECTS,
in the
BRITISH METROPOLIS & ITS VICINITY;
from Original Drawings by
Mr THOS H. SHEPHERD.
WITH
HISTORICAL, TOPOGRAPHICAL & CRITICAL ILLUSTRATIONS,
BY
James Elmes, M.R.I.A.

Left: A selection of designs for balconies, which were considered essential embellishments for the first floor of larger types of houses.

Chapter 1
The Architects and Their Styles

*'Each burst of house-building had a character of its own
– a different social character, representing a different
stratum of the national wealth and bringing into
prominence a different kind of taste.'*

William John Summerson, Georgian London
(London, Barrie & Jenkins, 1945, revised edition 1988)

Previous page: A particularly elaborate Classical scene fills the pediment of this building by John Nash (1752–1835), one of the greatest architects of his generation.

Above: Elevation of Eastbury in Dorset, the work of the architect and playwright Sir John Vanbrugh (1644–1726), as drawn by Colen Campbell in his *Vitruvius Britannicus* (Vol. I: 1715, Vol. II: 1717, Vol. III: 1725). Campbell's work, based on the ten-volume treatise *De architectura* of the Roman architect and engineer Vitruvius (fl. 1st century BC), contained easily copied models for a variety of Palladian building types, and was extremely influential in the revival of the Palladian style in eighteenth-century England.

Above: Interiors by Inigo Jones (1573–1652): left, a salon, right, a great dining room; drawings taken from Campbell's *Vitruvius Britannicus.*

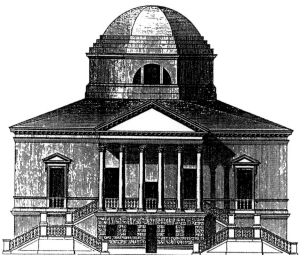

Left: Palladianism was introduced into England around 1715 and championed most keenly by the 3rd Earl of Burlington and 4th Earl of Cork, Richard Boyle (1694–1753). Lord Burlington's villa at Chiswick, 1725–9, designed by Inigo Jones, included notable features such as the so-called Diocletian or 'Thermal' window in the octagon and the prostyle hexastyle portico at the level of the *piano nobile* (principal, or first, floor).

Above: Whilst providing welcome shelter from the elements, porticos offered architects the opportunity to embellish appropriately an otherwise perhaps rather dull entrance, uplifting it to much grander proportions. These Corinthian columns enhance a residence in Virginia, USA, where the Georgian style took hold and in America is usually referred to as 'Colonial'.

Above: Decorum, correctness and above all a sense of proportion were essential features of Palladian architecture, shown here in a finely proportioned but severely Classical house in Regent's Park, London.

Left: The great sweep of the Royal Crescent, Bath, built 1767–c.75 by John Wood the Younger. A giant order of engaged Ionic columns rises from the *piano nobile* level to the crowning entablature. The Royal Crescent set the precedent for much ambitious urban design for nearly a century afterwards.

The Architects and Their Styles **19**

Design by Colen Campbell of 'the Great Hall of my Invention being a Cube of 40 feet'. Compare the marble hall at Clandon Park, Surrey.

Below: A ceiling design by Robert Adam, 1777. Ribbons, festoons and medallions were favourite Adam motifs.

Below: Some aspects of Kenwood House, north London, designed by Robert Adam (1728–92): columns of the Ionic order, delicate wrought-iron verandah supports and a Classically proportioned façade. Adam had measured ancient buildings in Italy and Spalato (now Split, in Croatia) and pioneered a Greek revival style, which was a move away from the Palladian interpretation of Classicism and a return to genuine Greek forms.

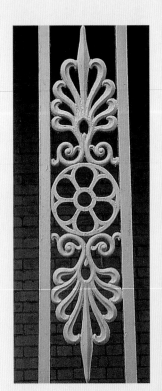

Above: Grovelands Priory, Southgate, north London was built in 1797–8 by John Nash. The house, with its Ionic columns, has been described as Nash's 'most scholarly tribute to neoClassicism'. The house was sited amid gardens landscaped by Humphrey Repton (1752–1818).

Right: Nash's attention to detail is evident in the simple but beautiful semicircular fanlight which nestles inside a recessed arch.

Right: A Chinese-style design for a summerhouse by Sir William Chambers (1723–96), designer of the famous Pagoda at Kew Gardens, London. Chambers wrote the seminal *Treatise on Civil Architecture* (1759), which remained influential well into the late Victorian era. Chinoiserie – the 'Chinese' style – became popular in both building and furniture design during the later Georgian period, or Regency, as it is often called.

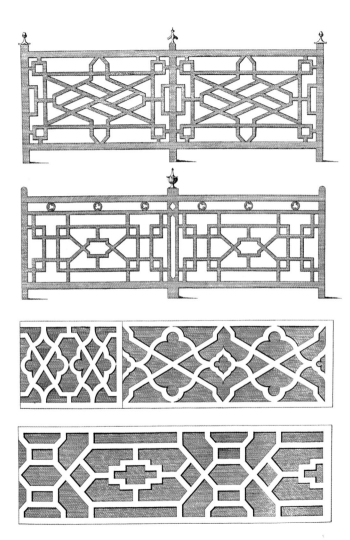

Left: Designs by Thomas Chippendale (1718 –79), cabinet-maker, upholsterer and author of T*he Gentleman and Cabinet-Maker's Director* (1754): the top two are for 'Chinese railings', the bottom two for 'Gothick frets'. The similarity is striking; both types of design were in favour during the Regency.

Below: An example of Georgian Gothick, which was a synthesis of Gothic, Chinese and decorative rococo styles. Turrets and pointed arches were hallmarks of Georgian Gothick.

Left and above: The Royal Pavilion at Brighton, commissioned by the Prince Regent from John Nash. Finished in 1821, the building was predominantly 'Hindoo' (Indian style) on the outside but Chinese on the inside, where the cast-iron staircases have balustrades in the form of bamboo lattice.

Right: Empire-style design for a ceiling by Percier and Fontaine – architects, designers and decorators to Napoleon. This style, which originated in France around the time of the first French empire, in fact represented a period longer than the duration of Napoleon's empire (1804–15). After the war with England of 1812–14, decorative features from continental Europe found their way to America.

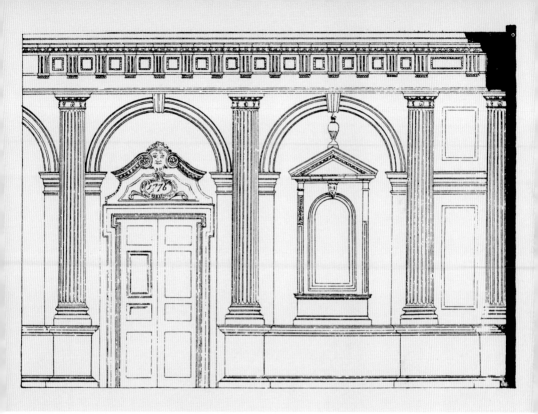

Above: View of the corridor of Independence Hall, Philadelphia, Pennsylvania, built by Andrew Hamilton and probably inspired by the architect James Gibbs (1682–1754), an important promulgator of forms through his books such as *Book of Architecture* (1728) and *Rules for Drawing the Several Parts of Architecture*, in which he simplified the rules of Palladianism so that they could be readily understood and used by builders.

Chapter 2
The Plan and Façade

*'Proportion is the first Principle, and proper Appropriation
of the parts constitute Symmetry and Harmony.'*

Robert Morris, 1751

Previous page: John Wood the Younger used a form derived from Druidical tradition, combined with half the elliptical plan of the Roman Coliseum, to create the majestic sweep of Bath's Royal Crescent.

Below: From the seventeenth century onwards British, and later American, architects emulated Classical styles. They were particularly drawn to the elegant austerity and precision of Greek columnar architecture, of which details of the three principal styles – Doric, Ionic and Corinthian – are illustrated here.

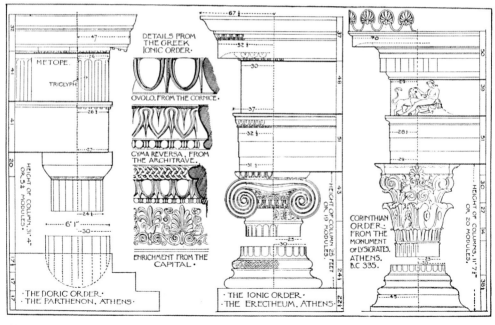

DETAILS FROM THE GREEK IONIC ORDER.

OVOLO. FROM THE CORNICE.

CYMA REVERSA, FROM THE ARCHITRAVE.

ENRICHMENT FROM THE CAPITAL.

METOPE.

TRIGLYPH

HEIGHT OF COLUMN, 31' 4" OR, 5¼ MODULES.

· THE DORIC ORDER ·
· THE PARTHENON, ATHENS ·

HEIGHT OF COLUMN 25 FEET OR, 19 MODULES.

· THE IONIC ORDER ·
· THE ERECTHEUM, ATHENS ·

CORINTHIAN ORDER: FROM THE MONUMENT OF LYSICRATES. ATHENS. B.C 335.

HEIGHT OF COLUMN, 11' 7½" OR, 20 MODULES.

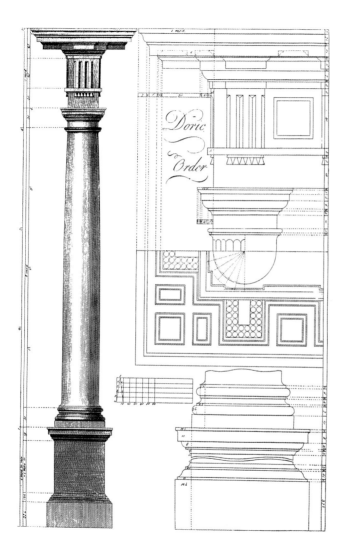

Doric Order

Left: Thomas Chippendale's famous *The Gentleman and Cabinet-Maker's Director* of 1754 was one of the first pattern books, which offered principles as well as practical designs for the builder, cabinet-maker or upholsterer.

Below: Typical examples of Georgian stone terraces in Bath, showing (below) classically pedimented doors and an iron railing fronting the basement 'area', as well as the sash windows that were considered a *sine qua non* throughout the Georgian period. The tallest windows are on the first floor, where the principal reception rooms tended to be situated.

Left: Classically proportioned terraced housing in Brighton, one of several seaside towns to be developed in the eighteenth century. The windows set into arched recesses add some interest to the otherwise starkly plain exterior.

Left: Typical Georgian stone terraces in Bath, with the tallest windows on the first floor and a row of dormers in the roof.

Right: In America, Georgian architecture inherited many ideas from Britain but also took other directions, influenced especially by Thomas Jefferson's own house, Monticello. Classical porticoes, as at this plantation house near Richmond, Virginia, became a feature of the grander country mansions, and later of more modest homes, too.

Above and right: The classical influences of ancient Greece are clearly evident in these designs for a window and a doorcase.

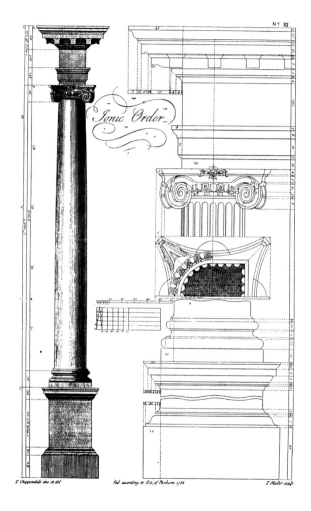

Ionic Order

T Chippendale inv et del   Pub according to Act of Parlum 1753   T Muller sculp

Left: Georgian architecture was based on the ancient system of Classical 'orders'. This engraving of the Ionic order is taken from Chippendale's *Gentleman and Cabinet-Maker's Director*.

Below: Rear view of London terraces, presenting a more confused exterior than the elegantly simple front elevations. In Georgian times roads were often artificially built up, while the rears of the building plots were at a lower level.

Above and left: Georgian terraces in London. All feature iron balconies, a raised front door, and iron railings separating the pavement from the sunken 'area' in front of the house.

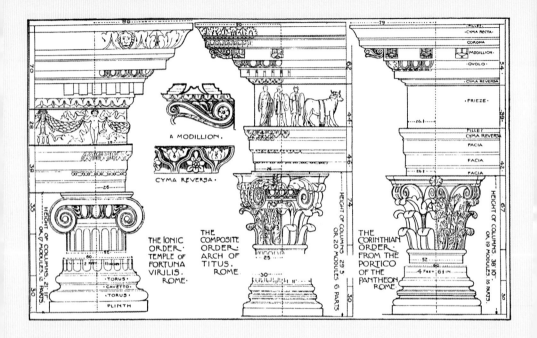

Above: Roman architecture was similar in plan to Greek but usually larger in scale and more ostentatious in its mouldings and ornaments. The Romans added the Tuscan and the Composite orders to the three existing orders.

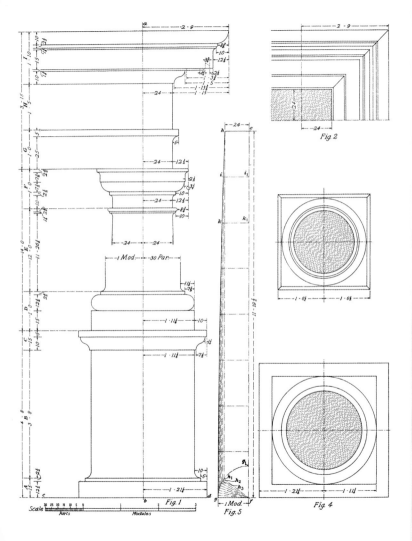

Fig. 2

Fig. 1

Fig. 4

Fig. 5

Scale
Parts
Modules

Left: The Tuscan was
the simplest of the five
Roman orders, and in
its original form was
probably an imitation
of the Greek Doric.

Left: Mathematical tiles became popular, particularly in fashionable seaside towns, as here, at Brighton, by the end of the eighteenth century. They were ceramic tiles with large pegs at the rear, which were nailed in overlapping layers on a vertical wall and resembled brick courses.

Left: The Georgian period was the time when fashionable seaside resorts such as Brighton (seen here) were laid out, very often in streets of brick terraces of three or more storeys. The palace-fronted terrace was conceived as a single, harmonious unit of rigid symmetricality; the example on the far left has an iron balcony running continuously along the façade.

Above: Unusual enclosed balconies above the porticoed entrances gave a wide view of the seafront in these attractive Brighton terraces.

Right: The Building Act of 1774 classified new houses into four types, called 'rates', in order to ensure sound construction and stringent fire-prevention measures. A house rated first class (right) was valued at over £850 and had a floor space of over 84 square metres (900sq ft).

Centre: Houses rated third and fourth class were the smaller types, worth, respectively, £150–£300 and less than £150, and occupying, respectively, 32–46 square metres (350–500sq ft) and less than 32 square metres (350sq ft). The dimensions of all rates of houses were standardized.

Far right: A house rated second class was worth between £350 and £850, in terms of its annual value in ground rent, and had a floor space of 46–84 square metres (500–900sq ft).

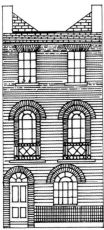

Below and right: The *piano nobile* (principal floor) was that on which the main reception rooms may have been situated, and received the most attention from architects.

Left: The curved bays on these Regency buildings in Brighton admitted plenty of light and gave unrestricted views to the residents.

Above left and right: Tall terraces with large windows, often within curved bays, were typical of Georgian seaside housing, as here at Brighton.

Right: Chippendale's *Director* illustrated the proportions and dimensions of the Corinthian order. The order was not much used by the Ancient Greeks, but it was characteristically refined and delicate in detail, and was thus an attractive model for Georgian architects.

Left: Features of the Corinthian order were the rich entablature; the deep and elaborate cornice; and the capital, a little greater than a diameter in height, and enriched with acanthus foliage and spiral volutes.

Far left: A monumental gateway frames and leads on to restrained terraces at Regent's Park, London.

Left: This building in Regent's Park, London, with its hexagonal tower above a pedimented doorway, borrows heavily from Classical models.

Above: Ornamented columns support the balcony of this imposing house situated in Regent's Park, London. The main window on the first floor is topped by a semicircular fanlight.

The Plan and Façade 51

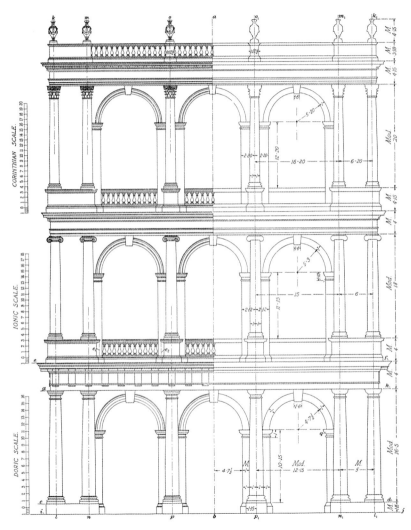

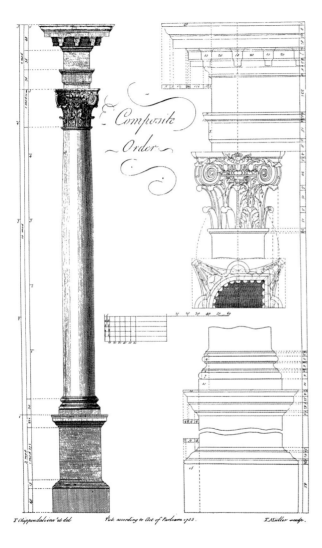

I Chippendale inv. et del   Pub. according to Act of Parliam 1753.   I Muller sculp.

Left: An extract from Chippendale's *Director* illustrating the Composite order, as used principally in the architecture of Italy.

Far left: In Roman amphitheatres and consequently in Georgian buildings, orders were sometimes placed above one another, an arrangement called superposition. The upper diameter of each shaft was made equal to the lower diameter of the one above it, as if they constituted a single tapering column.

Above: A 'house of parade', the grandest of Palladian house types, with an imposing columned portico framed by lower lateral wings.

Right: This house has a rigidly horizontal façade, with engaged columns which rise through two storeys, and also a starkly horizontal delineation between the upper storeys.

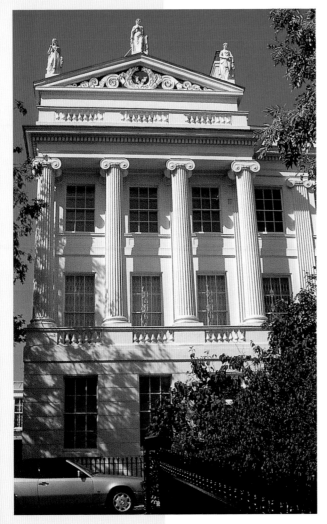

Left: Detached Ionic columns with their double scrolls support an elaborate pediment featuring a continuous frieze. The statues used in this order were often female figures clad in drapery which had vertical folds that echoed the flutings of the column.

Below: An interesting arrangement of windows adorns the façade of this house, including, on the top floor, a circular window called an oculus.

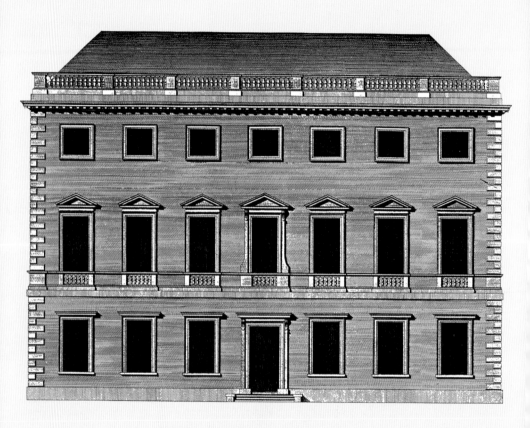

Above: Horizontal features, such as the stone courses
delineating the ground and first floors, demonstrate the
bare bones of Palladianism in the Duke of York's palace in
Pall Mall, London. Monotony was frequently a charge laid
against such buildings as the Georgian period wore on and
construction became standardized.

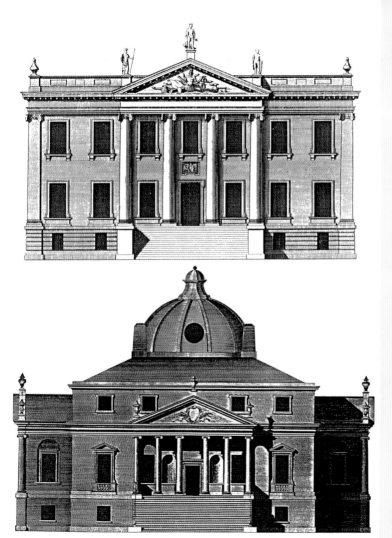

Left: An interesting example of the interplay between horizontal and vertical features in this Palladian-style house.

Left: Foots Cray, Kent, a typical Palladian house, with a columned portico which is reached by a flight of steps the height of the ground storey, also engaged columns at the extremities of the façade, and an oculus in the domed roof.

The Plan and Façade 57

Above: It was common practice for rural houses to be given two storeys, having tall rooms with symmetrically arranged sash windows.

Below: Venetian windows flanking the front door and arched windows on the first floor embellish this façade. The pediment over the door is unusual in that it is broken at the lower edge to make way for the arched fanlight.

Below: Whitewebbs House, on the outskirts of north London, features a recessed entrance and colonnaded wings. The roof is strewn with chimney stacks.

Above: The green of the front door was a popular feature of rural cottages in the Georgian period. Verdigris, a fine, deep green derived from corroding copper, was one of the more expensive oil-based paints.

Below and right: The rural houses shown here display a number of Georgian features, including Venetian (tripartite) windows, horizontal stone courses, an arched niche and a portico with triangular pediment.

Right: The roofed balcony is a delicate feature of this house situated in Kinsale, Southern Ireland. The façade, with its columns on the lower floors and two dormer windows, gives the impression of a triangle tapering towards the top.

Left: A house in Bristol with an unusual arched bay descending to the basement.

Right and below: External shutters frame the windows of these houses in Williamsburg, Virginia, USA; the dark colour of those on the house below is more likely to be authentic than the stark white seen on the left. Small Classical porticoes were favoured as a means of emphasizing the entrance.

Left and below: The Colonial style was the counterpart in North America of the Georgian style, with Palladian features such as regularly proportioned façades, sash windows and pedimented doorways. Roofs tended to be of steeper pitch than in England. Large central chimneys were also common.

Above: The east façade of the President's House, Washington DC, as it was in 1823. Thomas Jefferson (1743–1826), himself a distinguished architect, made many improvements to the house during his incumbency 1801–9, including the building of the terraces to accommodate the clerical offices, stables and servants' quarters.

Below: The garden elevation of the William Gibbes residence, Charleston, South Carolina, USA, built in 1775. The ground floor, which is bypassed by curving stairs, is clearly of secondary importance to the *piano nobile*, where the principal reception rooms were.

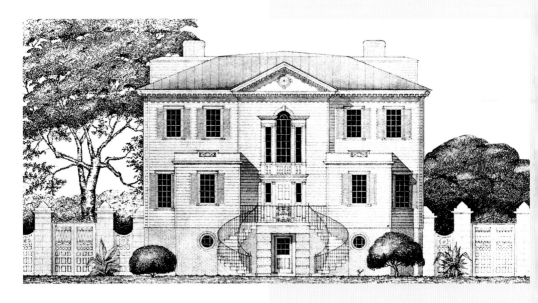

Below: Conventionally Classical columns,
embellished with scrolls and acanthus leaves.

Above: Details of columns in Georgian buildings, showing elongated scrolls (top right), Ionic double-paired scrolls (right), as at Kenwood House, north London, and the pared-down simplicity of the Tuscan order (above).

Right: A selection of some of the many designs for capitals and modillions (ornamental brackets) available to architects from pattern books of the time, both in Great Britain and in America.

Right: Venetian windows and large bow windows are typical Georgian features.

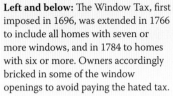
Left and below: The Window Tax, first imposed in 1696, was extended in 1766 to include all homes with seven or more windows, and in 1784 to homes with six or more. Owners accordingly bricked in some of the window openings to avoid paying the hated tax.

Left: With the improved production of glass, substantial glazing bars could be dispensed with, in favour of delicate wooden mouldings.

Left and below: Examples of windows, showing the diversity of designs. Pronounced bays were used in seaside towns to catch the sunlight radiating from the sea, but the bulging bow windows seen in modern mock-Georgian buildings never existed in Georgian times.

Left and below: There are Classical references in all these doors. The most understated – far left (top)– has panelling laid out in a way that echoes the sizes of windows in a Palladian house, the two tallest of six panels being in the centre and the two smallest at the top. Delicate patterns embellish the circular window and the fanlight in the door in the main picture.

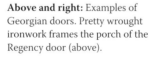

Above and right: Examples of Georgian doors. Pretty wrought ironwork frames the porch of the Regency door (above).

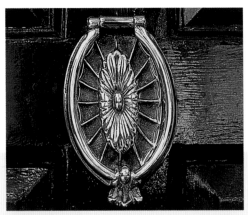

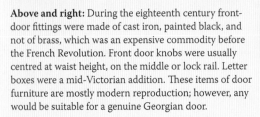

Above and right: During the eighteenth century front-door fittings were made of cast iron, painted black, and not of brass, which was an expensive commodity before the French Revolution. Front door knobs were usually centred at waist height, on the middle or lock rail. Letter boxes were a mid-Victorian addition. These items of door furniture are mostly modern reproduction; however, any would be suitable for a genuine Georgian door.

Below and right: Fanlights, which began to appear in the 1720s and were popular until the 1840s, allowed light to enter the hall or corridor behind the front door and also provided the designer with scope for invention. The circular window (right) has a simple geometric pattern of leading. The other three examples show some intricate designs.

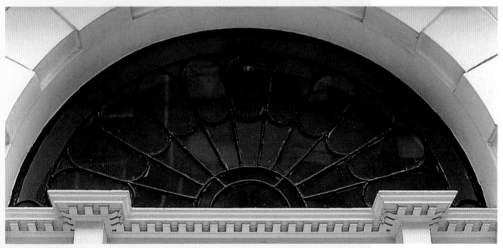

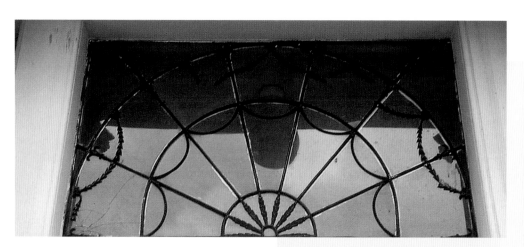

Some unusual fanlights. **Far top left:** a 'batswing' pattern, especially fashionable in the 1820s and 1830s, of essentially semicircular shape but set within a rectangular frame. **Far bottom left:** an example with a more flamboyant, heavier-handed design. **Left:** a bold and imposing oval light. **Below:** a glass pane echoing the keystone shapes on the door arch.

Right, below and overleaf:
A selection of the many types of decorative mouldings to be found ornamenting Georgian buildings. In the Georgian period these might be made of stucco, wood or stone, and consisted of various designs: spirals, cups, sheaths, rosettes, animal heads, birds, reptiles, scrolls, egg-and-dart designs, etc.

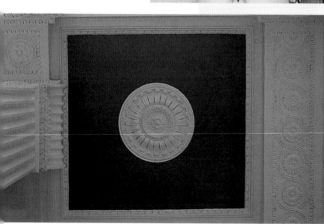

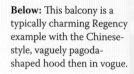

Below: This balcony is a typically charming Regency example with the Chinese-style, vaguely pagoda-shaped hood then in vogue.

Above: Iron balconies were becoming increasingly common by the 1780s, replacing the familiar iron window-guards. They were normally cantilevered out from the first floor and supported both by brackets on their undersides and by iron beams that extended far into the house. Many balconies on existing Georgian buildings are painted black; the original colour would probably have been green.

Right: Balconies might also have stone balustrades or demonstrate hybrid forms, combining Classical styles such as columns and pilasters with Georgian-period ironwork.

Right: Examples of decorative stone balcony supports, and finials used for garden walls.

Above and left: Crestings such as these would be found decorating the apex of a roof or, made of cast iron, as ornamentation added to window-sills.

Above and right: A variety of Georgian roofs and pediments. Tiles began to be superseded by slates, which permitted shallower roof pitches than tiles and were more efficient at keeping out rain. Diminishing courses of slates, as in the example at bottom right, were laid to transfer the bulk of the weight of the roof covering to the outer walls. It was fashionable to hide the roof itself from view at street level, by placing the roof-line parallel to a high, street-front parapet, as in some of the examples here (top left, top and middle right).

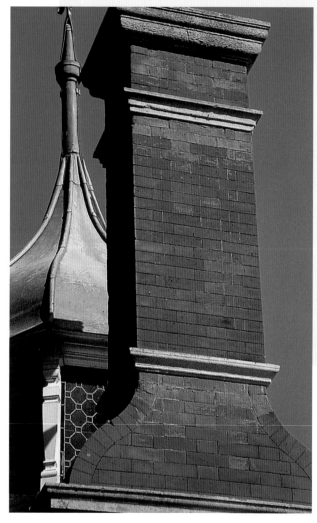

Above and right: The bulky chimneys, prominent dormer windows, onion domes and turrets and high parapets that were typical of the period; mansard roofs were also common. The roof above is an example of Georgian Gothick.

Below: Three examples of ironwork brackets used to support shelters to doorways.

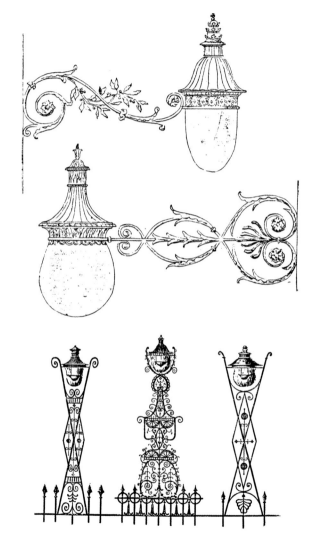

Left: Designs for ironwork lamp-holders, such as may be seen outside No. 10 Downing Street, London. These were published by Carter in 1750; two designs for ironwork lamp brackets, by Adam brothers, for Drapers Hall, London

Right: Cast- or wrought-iron balusters were becoming very common by 1800. Some might support a rail of mahogany. Decorative elements might be made of cast brass or lead. These examples are all open-string staircases, where the treads have been left exposed (sometimes, as in the example at the top of the page, elegantly carved). Where the balusters consisted of posts, these were often placed two, or even three to a stair.

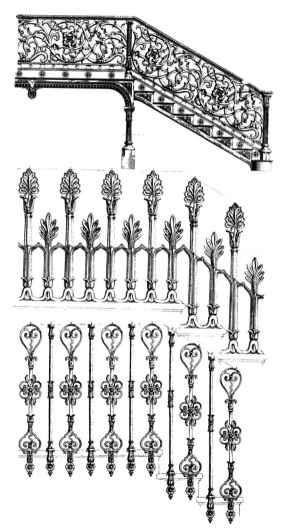

Below and right:
Examples of drainpipes, gutters and rainwater heads. Until about the end of the eighteenth century, these were made of softwood, sometimes lined with lead. Many later examples were made from cast iron. Lead was another commonly used roofing material.

Above and right: Iron boot-scrapers in various shapes and sizes, notably the lyre-shaped example (top right).

Below and opposite page: Early Georgian railings consisted of massive uprights terminating in spiked finials in the form of weapon heads. Through the eighteenth century, railings became more complex, lighter and more elaborately patterned (the patterns sometimes made of stamped or cast lead). Heart and honeysuckle (the classically derived anthemion) motifs were popularized by the Adam brothers. The examples on the right are from Great Ormond Street, London, and include a boot-scraper and a lamp support.

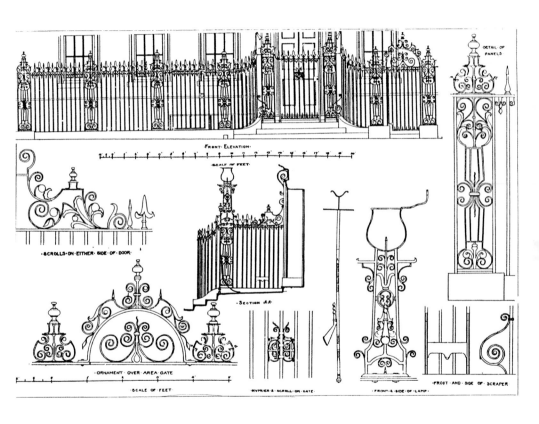

·FRONT·ELEVATION·

·SCALE·OF·FEET·

·SCROLLS·ON·EITHER·SIDE·OF·DOOR·

·SECTION·AA·

·DETAIL·OF·PANELS·

·ORNAMENT·OVER·AREA·GATE·

·SCALE·OF·FEET·

·NVPILEA·&·SCROLL·ON·GATE·

·FRONT·&·SIDE·OF·LAMP·

·FRONT·AND·SIDE·OF·SCRAPER·

Above and right: Georgian ironwork in both functional and decorative guises. Examples here include lamp holders, gates and gate posts, railings and finials.

Right: Wrought-iron gates such as the example shown here, were very fashionable for the grander Georgian houses.

Above: Garden gates at Scraptoft Hall, near
Leicester, designed by William Edney. The design
features a large central rosette and a scroll pattern
repeating four times; at the sides are pilasters with
lyre-motif fillings.

Chapter 3
Interiors and Furnishings

'Perhaps there is not a thing upon the face of the earth truer than the belief that taste is the general possession of all men; I mean every man assumes it to himself, tho' he denies it to his neighbour, by which it is at once universal in one view, and non-existent in another.'

John Shebbeare ('Battista Angeloni') (1709–88), letter to the Reverend Father Filippo Bonini in Rome, 1755, from Letters on the English Nation

Right and opposite page: Two chinoiserie designs for interiors by Sir William Chambers (1723–96). Chambers was born in Sweden of Scottish descent and had, unlike most of his contemporaries, actually visited China, where he became inspired by the Chinese style. Chinoiserie became very fashionable and was adopted by other architects and designers who also used it for furniture and whole buildings. It featured, for example, balconies covered by roofs of copper or lead, in emulation of the curved roof-line of a Chinese pagoda.

Previous page: The eighteenth-century dining room at Hatchlands, Surrey, is full of typical Robert Adam features, notably the ceiling and chimney breast ornament. He carried out the interior decoration in 1759 and it is his earliest known work in England. The house was built in 1756 by Admiral Boscawen, who defeated the French fleet at Louisberg in 1758.

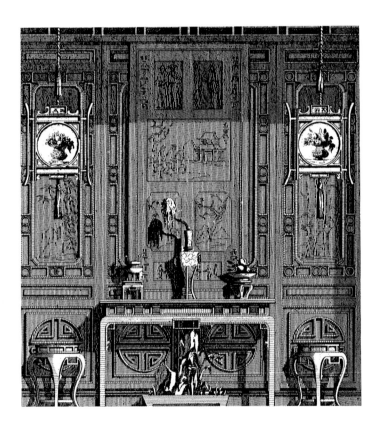

Far left: Since 1660 it had become important for all but the most modest houses to have a library; there was status to be had in owning one, even if it was filled with never-opened volumes or even – as sometimes happened – dummy books. The library fireplace at Hatchlands, Surrey (1758–61), includes round medallions and bas-reliefs of classical figures typical of Robert Adam's designs.

Left: This striking fireplace with its dominant Greek key design is further decorated with Bossi work – the technique of carving out white marble and infilling with decorative, coloured marble. Bartoli, an Italian craftsman of the period, was a master of this technique, and Robert Adam used his skills on a number of fireplaces.

Interiors and Furnishings 115

Above and opposite page, top: Designs for Georgian living rooms. Typical motifs were the swags below the ceiling cornice and above the door and the lyre shape in the chair backs. The furniture was probably of mahogany.

Left: A room designed by the architect Thomas Hope in 1807; it is described as 'in the Classic style', but represents the fashion for the Egyptian that was at its height between 1804 and 1810, probably as a result of Napoleon's Egyptian campaign. Even the chair arm-rests feature figures in the appropriate style.

Below: An elegant chimneypiece with fluted pilasters at the sides is a prominent feature of this room.

Right: The deep colour of the walls in this room at Hatchlands, Surrey, was typical of Georgian tastes. The fireplace is an original by Robert Adam.

Below: Dining-room furniture designed by Robert Adam, at Harewood House, Yorkshire. The house was built between 1759 and 1771 by John Carr of York for Edwin Lascelles, whose heir became the 1st Earl of Harewood. Robert Adam was responsible for the decoration of the house interior.

Above: A sideboard designed by Thomas Sheraton, 1793. The vase-like containers on the ends are knife-holders. Eighteenth-century dining rooms were used exclusively for dining, while the drawing room became the focus of the house. By the end of the century both drawing room and dining room were situated on the ground floor, a feature which continues to influence the design of houses today.

Above: The room of Mrs Fitzherbert (with whom George IV contracted a secret and invalid marriage in December 1785) at the Royal Pavilion, Brighton, Sussex.

Right: The designs of the wallpaper and furniture give this elegant dining room the feel of the chinoiserie style, popular in Georgian England.

Left and below: Typical designs for a variety of items of furniture and girandoles taken from the pattern books of: top, G. Thomas; below left, Hepplewhite; and below, Sheraton.

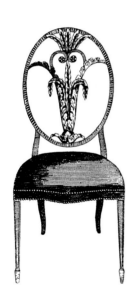

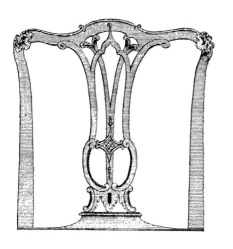

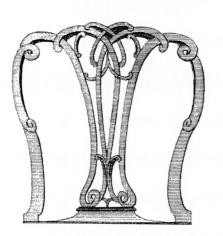

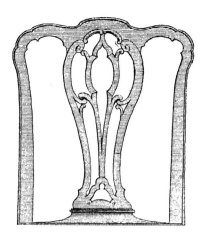

Left and below: Chairback designs by Thomas Chippendale. The central splat of carved openwork was a favourite with Chippendale.

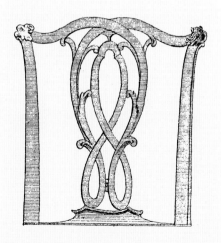

Left and below: Furniture design by Thomas Sheraton, c.1793. Sheraton was especially fond of the square-backed chair with a straight, horizontal top.

Right: A 'sofa table' design by Thomas Sheraton, 1804. This type of table, which had a flap at each end, was used as a writing table from c.1790.

Right: A Sheraton sideboard, made in mahogany, with brass rail and convex mirror at the back, 1802.

Right: Large pieces of furniture such as these bookcases by Adam (far right) and Sheraton (right), received the Classical treatment, their plain surfaces being embellished with pilasters and half-columns, mouldings and friezes and most of the other motifs and devices that were customarily seen on the buildings themselves.

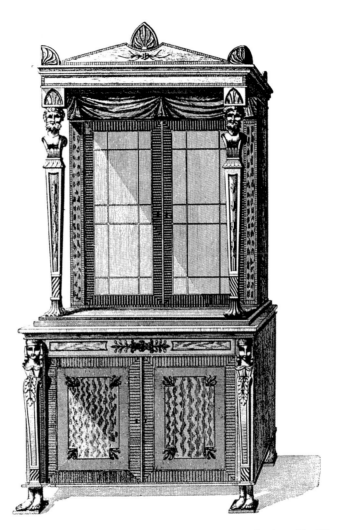

Left and below: Sofas from Chippendale's *The Gentleman and Cabinet-Maker's Director* (1754). His *Director* was the most comprehensive of numerous pattern books published from the 1740s onwards, and the first to be devoted to furniture alone.

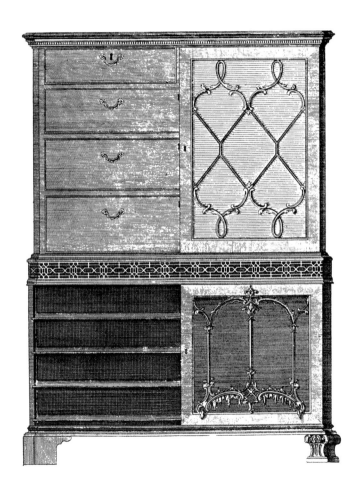

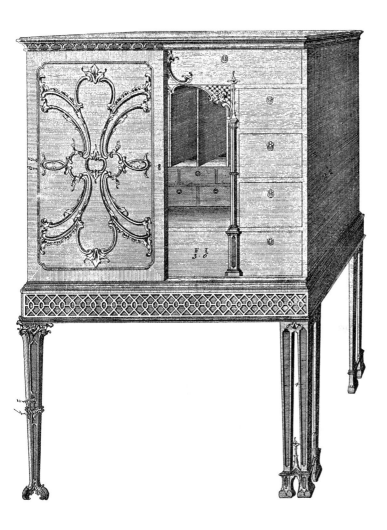

Right: Examples of chinoiserie designs by J Mayhew, Chippendale and William Chambers. Furniture in this style typically displayed a sharply angular lattice or trellis pattern. Little carved bells and angular peaks suggestive of pagodas were nearly always to be found, too. Chinese designs appeared on chairs, couches, tables and cabinets, as indeed they did on balustrades and other fixtures.

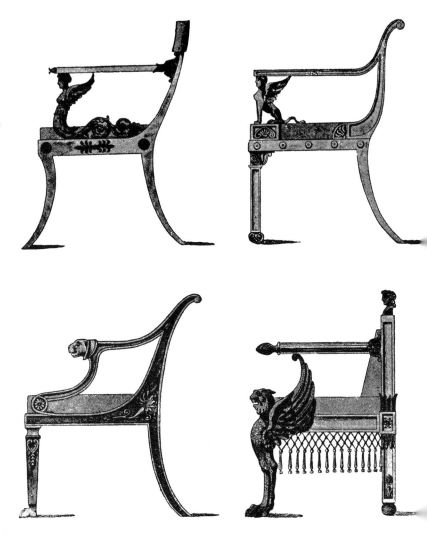

Right: Empire-style designs from George Smith's pattern book, *A Collection Of Designs for Household Furniture and Decoration*, 1808.

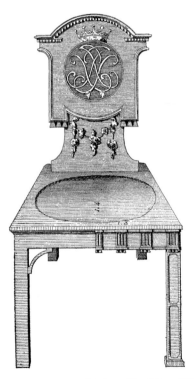

Below and left: Gothick designs from Chippendale. The Gothick craze developed from about the 1760s, and in furniture its presence is often recognizable by a pointed arch device.

Right and below:
Bedrooms and dressing rooms were often used for receiving visitors, and it was not unusual for the gentleman or lady of the house to entertain friends while actually in bed or while dressing. Bedrooms were assigned according to status, with the grandest being situated on the first floor, while servants were lodged in attics – or possibly in basements. Decorative schemes in bedrooms were lighter and more informal than in other reception rooms in the house, with blues and yellows being favoured.

Right: Traditional 'tester' beds, with four posts, or a solid headboard at the top end and two posts at the bottom, were common throughout the Georgian period.

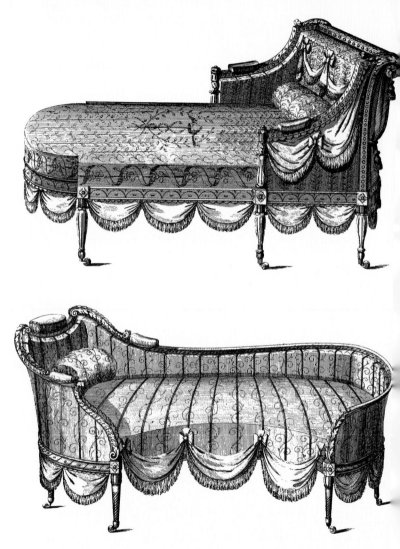

Left: Chaises longues designed by Thomas Sheraton. Items of furniture such as these might be found in the sitting room that often accompanied the main bedroom in grander houses.

Above: A Gothick-style bed designed by Thomas Chippendale.

Above: A bed in the grand manner, designed by Chippendale, 1759. Like many of the time, this bed had a headboard and two posts.

Right: A selection of designs for bedroom furniture to be found in pattern books. The designers of the period, notably Chippendale, Sheraton and Hepplewhite, included even the humble washstand in their style guides.

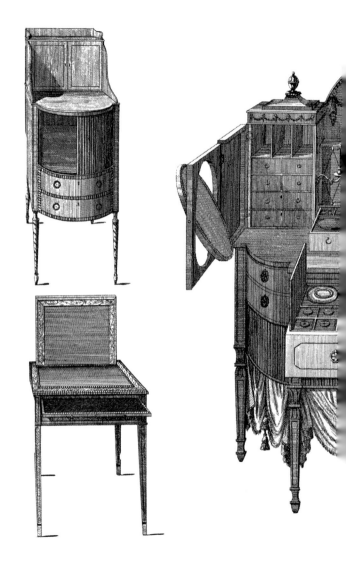

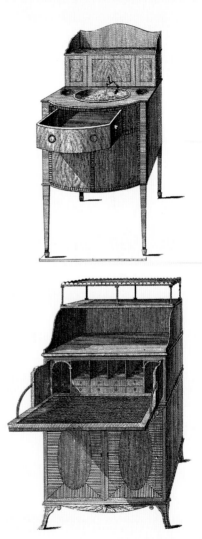

Left: Beds such as this carved oak example from the early Georgian period gave way to four-posters with elaborate headboards, which might be carved from pinewood and covered with material. The whole would be richly upholstered and hung with voluminous drapery. *Bylaw The Furniture Makers*

Below: A French design for a grand bedroom with built-in wardrobes and a bed which is set into an alcove.

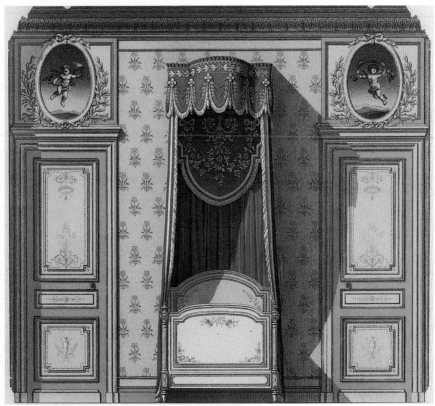

Left, right and overleaf: A selection of cooking stoves and utensils which might have been found in a Georgian kitchen. Kitchens in Georgian houses were purely functional, and kept at a distance from the rest of the house, sometimes in a basement or separate structure on the other side of a rear yard, or, in great houses, in an adjoining wing or a subsidiary building. The practice of cooking on the floor of an open hearth, and later on a grate, had given way by the middle of the eighteenth century to the use of appliances combining both oven and grate, and by the 1780s the enclosed cast-iron cooking range consisting of iron boiler, grate and oven had become the standard type, which continued in use until well into the twentieth century.

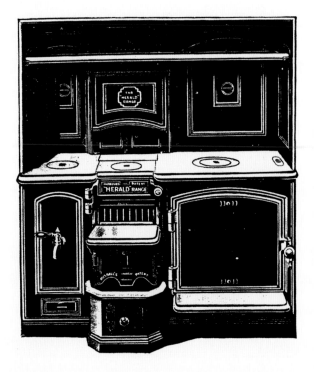

Above and far right: The dresser as we now think of it evolved during the eighteenth century from the court cupboards of the sixteenth century.
Bylaw The Furniture Makers

Left: A hand-painted Georgian-inspired kitchen, with a theme of eighteenth-century-style pilasters, cornices, mouldings and raised and fielded panels.

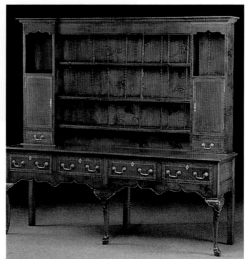

Right: A Georgian-style kitchen. The fittings may not be authentic, but the large central table was certainly regarded as an essential aid to food preparation at that time.

Above and top left: Kitchens of the period, such as these in Williamsberg, Virginia, USA, were purely functional with no pretensions to either beauty or elegance. The main items of furniture were the central table and one or more dressers for the storing of dry goods. The actual work surfaces were left unpainted and were cleaned by scrubbing.

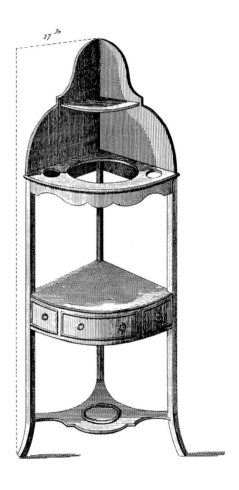

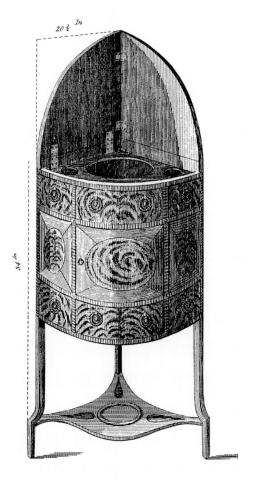

20 ¾ In

34 In

Left and overleaf: Bathing began to be popular in the late Georgian period, as technology brought improvements to sanitation. Public baths existed in London and some other cities; in some homes, plunge baths were carried into bedrooms and filled with water that had been heated in the kitchen. Sheraton produced a number of designs for toiletry equipment. Pieces such as these, including shaving tables and bidets – introduced from France – were used in dressing rooms in the better houses and discreetly disguised under and behind tops, shelves and other cabinetwork. The bedroom chamber pot was also concealed in a superior bedside table or cabinet.

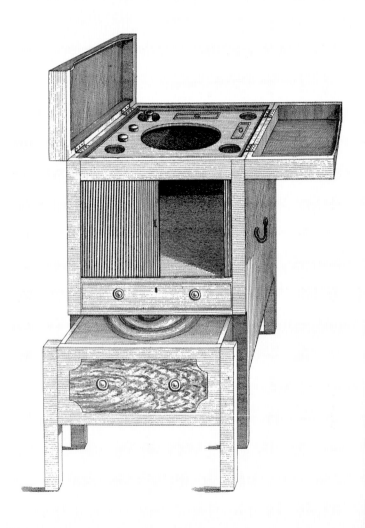

Chapter 4
Interior Details

*'Commenced taking off Roof of the House to be replaced
by a new one, to get rid of the evils of flat roofing and
spouts and gutters – or in other words, to supersede
the Jeffersonian by the Common Sense Plan.'*

*General John Hartwell Cocke, diary, 19 September 1836,
of his house Bremo, in Fluvanna County, Virginia, USA,
built in 1819 by Thomas Jefferson*

Previous page: By 1700 the six-panelled door had become standard both as a front door and within the home, where sometimes a four-panelled version was used. This classic example, with pilastered surround, was designed by William Kent.

Below: Georgian doors were nearly always painted; if not, they were polished with many layers of wax. The Georgians would have been shocked by the late twentieth-century fashion for stripped wood.

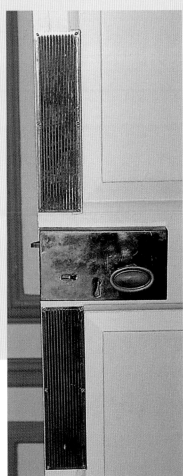

Left: A selection of interior doors with both functional and charmingly decorative door furniture.

Below and right: A range of designs for interior doors and doorcases from American pattern books, including those of Asher Benjamin. The door illustrated right demonstrates typical Palladian proportions.

Above and far right: By 1700 sash windows in Britain were fitted with interior shutters, which were often horizontally divided into two or three separately hinged sections. Opening the top section only allowed some daylight in, while protecting furniture and fittings from damaging direct light. External shutters were also common, few of which have survived in Britain today; although they can still be seen in the United States.

Left: Full-length, arch-topped windows admit maximum light to a living room.
Haddonstone

Left: A selection of designs for window treatments from pattern books of the period. Full window curtains replaced simple cloth hangings in the early Georgian period in finer houses only, but by the 1730s they were a feature of every domestic interior. By 1765, in the words of Benjamin Franklin, the fashion was 'to make one Curtain only for each window'. Roller blinds were also used in this period.

Above and right: Designs for window treatments from Chippendale (above) and Sheraton (right).

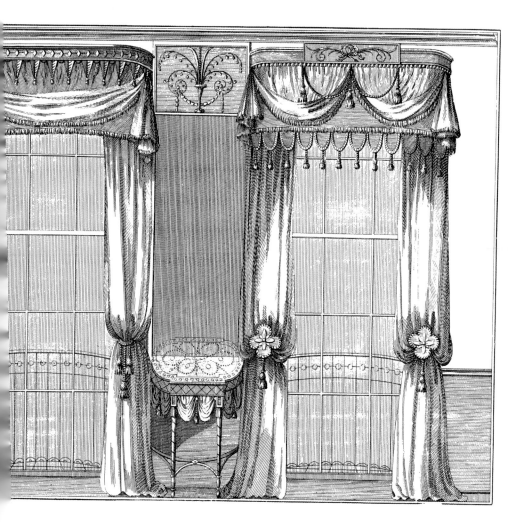

Right: An attractive modern interpretation of Georgian-style curtains, wallpaper and upholstery fabric. *Sandersons*

Left: Modern interior fabrics in the Regency style. *Sandersons*

Left: A range of typical plaster mouldings. Palladian architects introduced hand-modelled plasterwork and plaster wall panels derived from French patterns. However, most house-owners could not afford such individual treatment and so pre-moulded ornament was applied to the finished plaster wall.

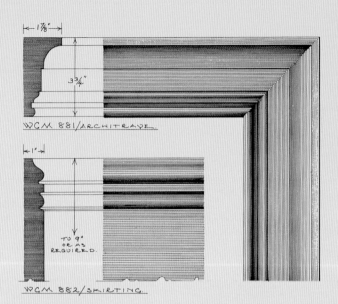

← 1⅞″ →

3¾″

WCM 881/ARCHITRAVE.

← 1″ →

TO 9″
OR AS
REQUIRED.

WCM 882/SKIRTING.

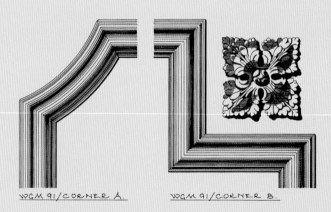

WCM 91/CORNER A.

WCM 91/CORNER B.

WGM 91/CORNER A. WGM 91/CORNER B.

U. 94

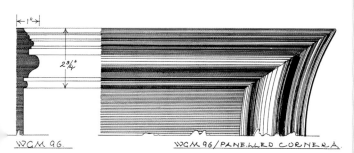

|← 1" →|

2 3/4"

WGM 96. WGM 96/PANELLED CORNER A.

U. 95

95/CORNER A.

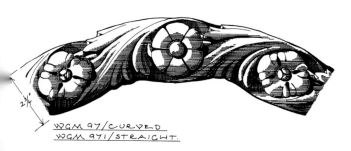

2 3/4"

WGM 97/CURVED
WGM 971/STRAIGHT.

Below and right: From the eighteenth century, alcoves on either side of the fireplace were turned into niches with plasterwork tops in imitation of styles in the larger houses.

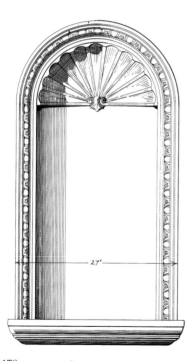

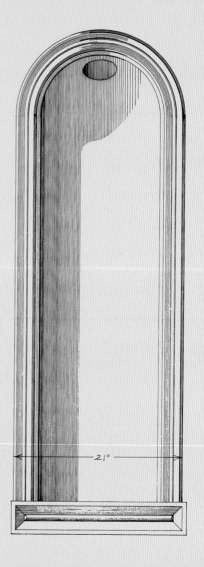

27'

21"

Above: Wallpapers which reflect the
Georgian predilection for oriental design.

Left: The plush Green Drawing Room at Clandon Park, Surrey, has plasterwork by the Italian stuccoers Artari and Bagutti. Above the marble fireplace is a panel with a painted classical scene. The wallpaper dates from 1735; by the late seventeenth century, luxury wallpaper was being imported from China. More commonly in the eighteenth century, walls were painted, with pastel shades being preferred, although green and red were popular colours for dining rooms and libraries.

Right: Designs for cornices, dados and other plasterwork could be quite elaborate, with motifs even picked out in gilt, although most plaster mouldings were painted white or, more often, the same colour as the flat ground. In general, moulded plasterwork was more plentiful and more decorative in the rooms that were likely to be on show; thus modest rooms had only rudimentary mouldings.

Left: Empire-style stencilled border for walls and cornices. In America, stencilling in distemper was extremely popular, particularly for floorboards and walls.

Below: Designs by Thomas Chippendale of 'borders for damask or paper hangings', 1761.

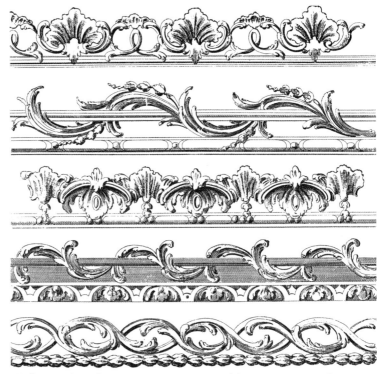

T. Chippendale inv.t et delin.   *Publish'd according to Act of Parliam.t 1761.*   *Clowes Sculp.*

Right: Delft tiles such as those shown here, were frequently used in fire surrounds. These are of English origin and date from around the middle of the eighteenth century.

Left and below: Carpets were used in wealthy homes – carpet manufacture in Britain was boosted after the Industrial Revolution – but alternatives included solid floors with inlaid mosaic tiles or stencilled designs. Portland stone, marble, slate and timber were popular materials.

Right and overleaf:
A range of cornices, roses and ornamented ceilings. Plasterwork on ceilings continued to be highly decorative in Palladian houses in Britain and America until the mid-eighteenth century, and was much sought after in all grades of Georgian house.

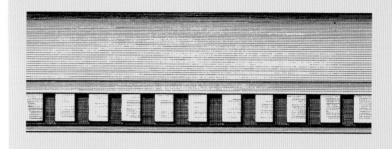

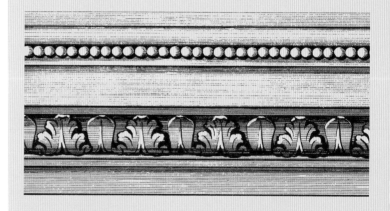

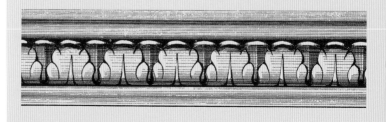

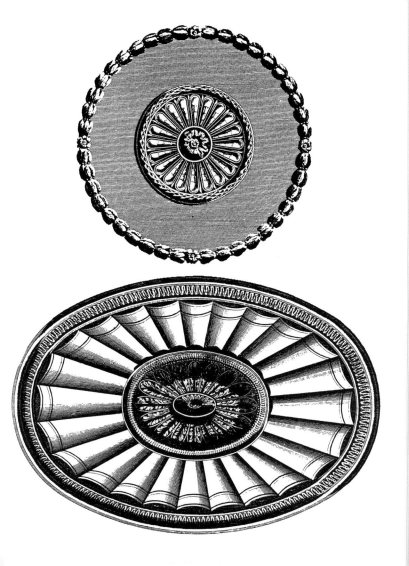

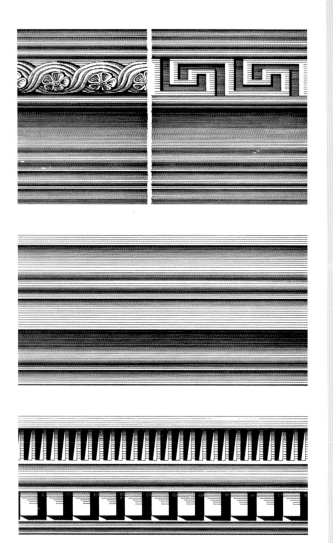

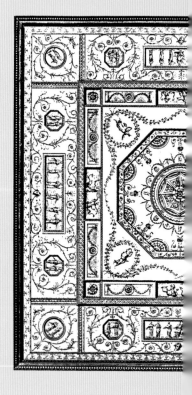

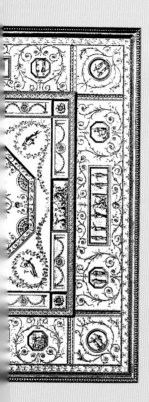

Right: Moulded plaster decoration was often confined to the cornice, although showier houses displayed profuse and lavish ornament, with stuccoed and painted ceilings.

Above and right: Two highly decorated ceilings in the style of Robert Adam (above) and Louis XV (right).

Above: Georgian staircases with elaborate iron openwork, ending in a scroll on the bottom step.

Below and right: Turned wooden balusters and (below) carved handrails curving around the newel post. Two or even three balusters to a tread were popular throughout the eighteenth century.

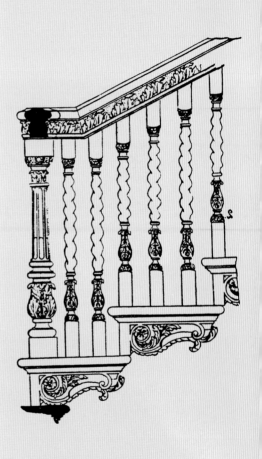

Below and right: Very decorative wrought-iron balusters embellish these staircases.

Below and right: Chandeliers can look splendid – the grandest were called 'lustres' – but the light the original ones afforded was often inadequate. The example on the right hangs in the Palladio Room at Clandon Park, Surrey, which also features a marble fireplace and French flock wallpaper from 1780.

Right and overleaf:
A range of light fittings of various degrees of elaborateness from pattern books of the period. Through most of the Georgian period homes were lit either by candles or by gas lamps, and in most cases the lighting arrangements were far more aesthetically pleasing than they were functional; houses in both America and Britain were, by modern standards, seriously underlit.

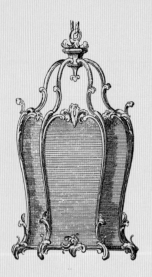

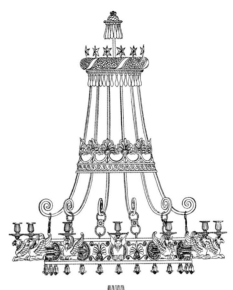

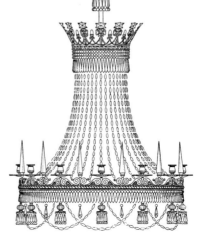

Left and above: From the 1720s the 'stove grate' was gradually replaced by the 'hob grate'. Both consisted of a free-standing, rectangular basket with fire bars and a grid for falling ash at the bottom, but the hob grate had flat-topped hobs flanking the basket. The chimneypieces on these pages display many splendid Georgian features, including marble inset, keystone, fluted pilasters and stylish fireplace furniture. Above is an example from Williamsberg, Virginia, USA.

Above and far right: The Coalbrookdale or Carron Company, of which John Adam was a partner, manufactured cast-iron surrounds, grates, fenders and fire-irons.

Left: An Adam-style mantelpiece incorporating Bossi work: white marble, carved out and infilled with decorative, coloured marble. The club fender provides additional seating for more relaxed gatherings by this otherwise formal fireplace.

Left and overleaf: Two stove grates (left) for burning logs, and a selection of chimneypieces. As the Georgian period wore on, chimneypieces, once very ornate and decorated with bucolic scenes, began to develop along simpler, more Classical lines.

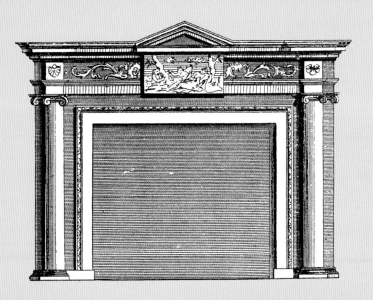

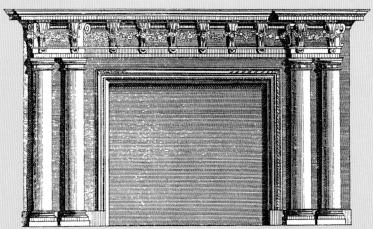

Chapter 5
The Garden

'The works of a person that builds, begin immediately to decay;
while those of him who plants begin directly to improve.'

William Shenstone (1714–63),
Unconnected Thoughts on Gardening

Above: Eighteenth-century garden designers such as William Kent (1685–1748), Charles Bridgeman (d.1738) and James Gibbs (1682–1754), would often station eye-catching features – like this Classical-style 'temple' – in the vistas they were aiming to create.

Previous page: An informal garden of the kind early Georgian gardeners tried to achieve by 'improving' the natural environment, with ornamental lakes and waterways and careful plantings of trees.

Below: This conservatory would afford attractive views from within as well as making a pretty addition to the house when seen from the garden. *Oak Leaf Conservatories*

SQUARE →

Left and overleaf: Examples of topiary and designs for elaborate clipped hedges for the grander garden, from a pattern book of the period.

Right: A chinoiserie garden pavilion designed by William Chambers, who was also responsible for the famous pagoda in Kew Gardens, London, where he claimed he had made an Eden out of 'what was once a Desert'.

Below: Sir Uvedale Price (1747–1829), an advocate of the Picturesque movement, drew up tables of levels of picturesqueness – for instance, ruins were considered more picturesque than cottages.

Above: In many great gardens of the early eighteenth century, avenues of trees were trained by pleaching (tying new growths to horizontal wires attached to tall poles).

Left: Statues were not merely decorative but, with their Classical allusions, were intended to have intellectual appeal to people of education and discernment.

Centre: A stone urn at the junction of paths sets off the lawn on one side and the massed plantings on the other.

Above: A ha-ha, a sunken ditch that served as an effective barrier to animals but did not disrupt the vista.

Right: Designs for garden buildings, all in the Gothick style. By this period, the main reason behind their creation was more to surprise and amuse than to provide sensible garden rooms.

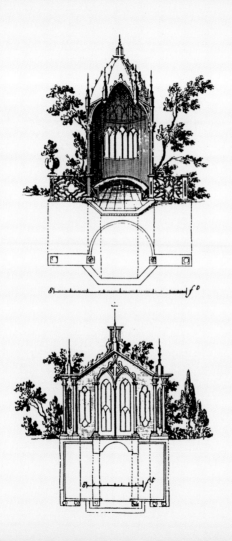

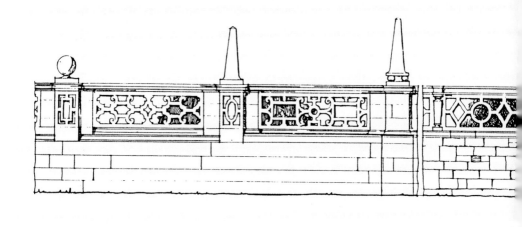

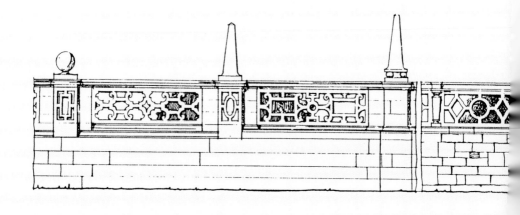

Left: Designs for terrace walls and balustrades, featuring examples of balusters, arcades, piers and tiles. Brick, with concrete filling, wood and stone were preferred materials.

Below: Some designs for extravagantly ornamented garden seats by Thomas Chippendale, 1761.

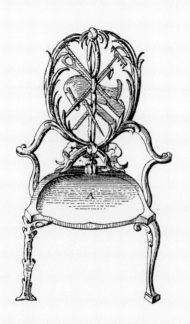

Stockists

The lists of suppliers given on these pages cannot be exhaustive and are intended only as a starting point. The Internet, local papers and commercial telephone directories are always worth looking at and are good sources of information about your own area. Alternatively there are many organizations giving specialist information and advice and those who will search for specific items.

UNITED KINGDOM

Information & Advice

Architectural Salvage
Netley House
Gomshall
Guildford, Surrey GU5 2QA
Tel: 01483 203221
www.handr.co.uk
Index of architectural items.
For a fee they will
put buyers in touch with
sellers. They do not keep
items for sale.

The Brooking Collection
School of Architecture/
Construction
University of Greenwich
Avery Hill Campus
Mansion Site, Bexley Road
London SE9 2PQ
Tel: 020 833 19312
www.dartfordarchive.org.uk
Unique record of the
development of period detail.
Information and advice
available.

English Heritage
Customer Services
Department
PO Box 569
Swindon
Wiltshire, SN2 2YP
Tel: 0870 333 1181
www.english-heritage.org.uk
Provides specialist and

technical advice on repair, maintenance and preservation; also gives grants for repairing historic buildings throughout England.

The Georgian Group
6 Fitzroy Square
London W1T 5DX
Tel: 08717 502936
www.georgiangroup.org.uk
Gives advice on repair and restoration to owners of Georgian buildings.

The Guild of Master Craftsmen
Castle Place, 166 High Street
Lewes
East Sussex BN7 1XU
Tel: 01273 478449
www.guildmc.com
Trade association putting prospective clients in touch with experienced craftsmen able to carry out restoration work. Also publishes Guide to Restoration Experts.

The Society for the Protection of Ancient Buildings
37 Spital Square
London E1 6DY
Tel: 020 7377 1644
www.spab.org.uk
Issues technical publications on historic buildings repairs and can supply names of specialist architects and other professionals.

Architectural Antiques & Reproductions

Architectural Antiques
70 Pembroke Street
Bedford, Bedfordshire
MK40 3RQ
Tel: 01234 213131
www.heritagebritain.com

Architectural Rescue 2
13 Southampton Way
Camberwell
London SE5 7SW
Tel: 020 7277 0081

Bailey's Architectural
Salvage
Whitecross Farm, Bridstow
Ross-on-Wye
Herefordshire HR9 6JU
Tel: 01989 563015

Brighton Architectural
Salvage
33–34 Gloucester Road
Brighton BN1 4AQ
Tel: 01273 681656

Britain's Heritage
Shaftsbury Hall
3 Holy Bones
Leicester LE1 4LJ
Tel: 01162 519592
www.britainsheritage.com

Cranborne Stone
West Orchard
Shaftesbury
Dorset SP7 OLJ
Tel: 01258 472685
www.cranbornestone.com

D & P Theodore
Reclamation
North Road
Bridgend Industrial Estate
Bridgend
Glamorgan CF31 3TP
Tel: 01656 648936

Edinburgh & Glasgow
Architectural Salvage Yards
31 West Bowling Street
Leith EH6 5NX
Tel: 01315 547077
www.salvoweb.com

Haddonstone Ltd
The Forge House
East Haddon
Northampton NN6 8DB
Tel: 01604 770711
www.haddonstone.co.uk

Shiners
123 Jesmond Road
Jesmond
Newcastle-upon-Tyne
Tel: 01912 816474

Solopark Ltd
The Old Railway Station
Station Road
near Pampisford
Cambridgeshire CB2 4HB
Tel: 01223 834663
www.solopark.co.uk

Walcot Reclamation
l08 Walcot Street
Bath
Avon BA1 5BG
Tel: 01225 444404
www.walcot.com

Warehouse Antiques
17 Wilton Street
Holderness Road
Hull
Tel: 01482 326559
www.warehouseantiques.
inc.com

Conservatories
Amdega Ltd
Faverdale Industrial Estate,
Darlington

Co Durham DL3 OPW
Tel: 01325 468522
www.amdega.co.uk

Goldcrest Windows &
Conservatories
Stone Lane Industrial Estate
Wimborne
Dorset BH21 1HB
Tel: 01202 885884
www.goldcrest-windows.
com

Classical Conservatories
Unit 16c
Chalwyn Industrial Estate
St Clements Road
Poole
Dorset BHI5 3PE
Tel: 01202 733001

Malbrook Conservatories
2 Crescent Stables
139, Upper Richmond Road
London SW15 2TN
Tel: 020 878 05522
www.malbrook.com

Oak Leaf Conservatories Ltd
Kettlestring Lane
Clifton Moor
Industrial Estate
North Yorkshire YO30 4XF
Tel: 01904 690401
www.oakleafconservatories.
co.uk

Vale Garden Houses Ltd
Belton Park, Londonthorpe
Road
Grantham, Lincolnshire
NG31 9SJ
Tel: 01476 564433
www.valegardenhouses.com

Doors & Windows
Bradford and Sestini
The Old Engine House
Hall Farm, Main Street
Kirklington, Newark
Notts NG22 8NN
Tel: 01636 816415

Copycats
The Workshop

29 Maypole Road
Ashurst Wood
East Grinstead
West Sussex RH19 3QN
Tel: 01342 811140
www.copycat1.freeuk.com

Fineline Traditional Joinery
Honeybridge Mushroom
Farm, Honeybridge Lane
Dial Post, Horsham
West Sussex RH13 8NX
Tel: 01403 711530
www.fine-line.demon.co.uk

Indoors Ltd
Beechin Wood Lane
Platt, Sevenoaks
Kent TN15 8QN
Tel: 01732 887445
www.indoorsltd.co.uk

The London Door Company
155 St John's Hill
London SW11 1TQ
Tel: 020 7801 0877
www.londondoor.co.uk

Restoration Windows
Unit 5, Bell Industrial Estate
Cunnington Street, Chiswick
London W4 5HB
Tel: 020 8742 1122
www.restorationwindows.
co.uk

The Sash Window
Workshop
Unit 4, Kiln Lane
Bracknell,
Berkshire RG12 1NA
Tel: 0800 597 2598;
01344 868668
www.sashwindow.com

Henry Venables Timber Ltd
Tollgate Drive,
Tollgate Industrial Estate
Stafford ST16 3HS
Tel: 01785 270600
www.henryvenables.com

Door Furniture

Architectural Components
Ltd

Locks & Handles and
Interiors of South
Kensington
4–8 Exhibition Road
London SW7 2HF
Tel: 020 7581 2401
www.doorhandles.co.uk

Beardmore Architectural
Ironmongery
321 Fulham Road
London SW10 9QL
Tel: 020 7351 5444
www.beardmore.co.uk

Brass Tacks Fittings Ltd
8 Kildare Close
Ruislip,
Middlesex HA4 9LG
Tel: 020 8866 8664
www.brasstacksfittings.co.uk

Clayton-Munroe Ltd
15–20 Burke Road
Totnes Industrial Estate
Totnes
Devon TQ9 5XL

Tel: 01803 865700
www.claytonmunroe.com

The Fingerplate Company
The Limes, Coles Oak Lane
Dedham, Colchester
Essex CO7 6DR
Tel: 08707 650100
www.fingerplates.com

The Period House Group
Anvil House,
129 Westgate Road
Belton, Doncaster DN9 1QA
Tel: 0845 602 3402
www.phg-uk.com

Fabrics & Wallpapers

Alexander Beauchamp
The Printworks, Hall Lane
Rhos, Wrexham LL14 1TG
Tel: 01978 844488
www.alexanderbeauchamp.
com

Cole & Son (Wallpapers) Ltd
Ground Floor 10, Chelsea

Harbour Design Centre
Lots Road,
London SW10 0XE
Tel: 020 7376 4628
www.cole-and-son.com

Colefax and Fowler
North Room,
39 Brook Street
London W1K 4JE
Tel: 020 7493 2231
www.colefax.com

Hamilton Weston
Wallpapers Ltd
18 St Mary's Grove
Richmond
Surrey TW9 1UY
Tel: 020 8940 4850
www.hamiltonweston.com

Ornamenta
George Spencer Designs,
33 Elystan Street
London SW3 3NT
Tel: 020 7591 0077
www.ornamenta.co.uk

Sanderson & Sons
Unit G9,
Chelsea Harbour
Design Centre
Lots Road,
London SW10 0XE
Tel: 08708 300066
www.sanderson-uk.com

Zoffany
Chelsea Harbour
Design Centre
Lots Road,
London SW10 0XE
Tel: 08708 300066
www.zoffany.co.uk

Fireplaces

Aga (formerly
Coalbrookdale)
Glynwed Consumer &
Building Products Ltd
Station Road, Ketley
Telford,
Shropshire TFI 5AQ
Tel: 01952 642000
www.aga-rayburn.co.uk

Adrian Ager Ltd (formerly
Ashburton Marbles)
38 North Street
Ashburton
Devon TQ13 7QD
Tel: 01364 653189
www.afager@tinyworld.
co.uk

Antique Fireplace Centre
30 Molesworth Road, Stoke
Plymouth, Devon PL1 5NA
Tel: 01752 559441

Chesney's Antique Fireplace
Warehouse
194–202 Battersea Park
Road
London SW11 4ND
Tel: 020 7627 1410

Chiswick Fireplace
68 Southfield Road
Chiswick, London W4 1BD
Tel: 020 8995 4011
www.thechiswickfireplace.
co.uk

Club Fenders from Acres
Farm
Bradfield
Berkshire, RG7 6JH
Tel: 01189 744305
www.acresfarm.co.uk

James Gray & Son Ltd
89 George Street
Edinburgh EH2 3EZ
Tel: 01312 257381
www.graysofedinburgh.co.uk

Marble Hill Fireplaces Ltd
70–72 Richmond Road
Twickenham
Middlesex TW1 3BE
Tel: 020 8892 1488
www.marblehill.co.uk

Jonathan Murray Fireplaces
358 Upper Richmond Road
East Sheen
London SW14 7JT
Tel: 020 8876 7934

Rockingham Fender Seats
Grange Farm, Thorney
Peterborough PE6 0PJ
Tel: 01733 270233
www.rockingham-
fenderseats.com

Townsend's Fireplaces
81 Abbey Road
St John's Wood
London NW8 0AE
Tel: 020 7624 4756

Kitchens
Bygone Ltd
Fieldside Farm, Quainton
Aylesbury
Bucks HP22 4DQ
Tel: 01296 655573

Bylaw The Furniture Makers
The Workshop
Norwich Road, Lenwade
Norfolk NR9 5SH
Tel: 01603 308090
www.bylaw.co.uk

Chalon UK Ltd
Hambridge Mill
Hambridge
Langport
Somerset TA10 0BP
Tel: 01458 254600
www.chalon.com

Naturally Wood
3 Twyford Road
Bishops Stortford
Hertfordshire CM23 3JL
Tel: 01279 755501
www.naturallywood.co.uk

Newcastle Furniture
Company
Unit 15
Fairfield
Industrial Park
Bill Quay, Gateshead,
Tyne & Wear NE10 0UW
Tel: 01914 699001
www.newcastlefurniture.com

Robinson & Cornish
St George's House
St George's Road
Barnstaple
Devon EX32 7AS
Tel: 01271 329300
www.robinsonandcornish.
co.uk

Mark Wilkinson
Furniture Ltd
Overton House
High Street, Bromham
Nr. Chippenham
Wiltshire SN15 2HA
Tel: 01380 850007
www.mwf.com

Smallbone of Devizes
Showrooms: Devizes,
Edinburgh, London,
Glasgow, Harrogate,
Knutsford, Leamington Spa,
St Albans, Sunningdale,
Tunbridge Wells
Tel: 020 7589 5998
www.smallbone.co.uk

Kitchen Ranges
Aga-Rayburn
Aga, Station Road
Ketley, Telford
Shropshire TF1 5AQ
Aga Tel: 08457 125207
Rayburn Tel: 08457 626147
www.aga-rayburn.co.uk

Architectural Heritage of
Northants
Taddington Manor
Taddington, Nr. Cutsdean
Cheltenham
Gloucestershire GL54 5RY
Tel: 01386 584414
www.architectural-heritage.
co.uk

Country Cookers
Unit LB4, Cattle Market
Hereford HR4 9HX
Tel: 01432 342351

Wye Valley Heating Centre
23 Station Street,
Ross-on-Wye

Herefordshire HR9 7AG
Tel: 01989 567003

Yorkshire Range Company
Japonica, Chapel Lane
Halton East, Skipton
North Yorkshire BD23 6EH
Tel: 01756 710263
www.yorkshirenet.co.uk/
yorkshirerangecompany

Lighting
Best & Lloyd Ltd
2 Holly Road, Edgbaston
Birmingham, West Midlands
B15 2UP
Tel: 01214 556400
www.bestandlloyd.co.uk

R & J Chelsom & Co Ltd
Heritage House
Clifton Road
Blackpool
Lancashire FY4 4QA
Tel: 01253 831400
www.chelsom.co.uk

Lights on Broadway
64 East Street, Brighton
West Sussex BN1 1HQ
Tel: 01273 737335
www.lightsonbroadway.com

Magic Lanterns By George!
23 George Street
St Albans, Herts AL3 4ES
Tel: 01727 865680

Olivers Lighting Company
Bideber Mill
Westhouse, Ingleton
Carnforth
North Yorkshire LA6 3NY
Tel: 01524 242478
www.oliverslighting.co.uk

Albert Bartram
177 Hivings Hill
Chesham, Bucks HP5 2PN
Tel: 01494 783271
www.ravencom.demon.co.uk

Starlite Chandeliers Ltd
Gibraltar House, Rodd

Industrial Estate, Govett
Avenue, Shepperton
TW17 8AB
Tel: 020 820 67500
www.impexglass.co.uk

Sugg Lighting
Sussex Manor Business Park
Gatwick Road, Crawley
West Sussex RH10 9GD
Tel: 01293 540111
www.sugglighting.co.uk

Christopher Wray Lighting
600 King's Road
London SW6 2YU
Tel: 020 775 18701
www.christopherwray.com

Metalwork
Beardmore Architectural
Ironmongery
321 Fulham Road
London SW10 9QL
Tel: 020 7351 5444
www.beardmore.co.uk

Bishopsbourne Forge
Bishopsbourne
Canterbury CT4 5HT
Tel: 01227 830784

Britannia Architectural
Metalwork Ltd
The Old Coach House
Draymans Way
Alton
Hampshire GU34 1AY
Tel: 01420 84427
www.britannia.uk.com

Colston Forge
Colston Yard, Colston Street
Bristol BS1 5BD
Tel: 01179 273660
www.colston-forge.co.uk

Dorothea Restorations Ltd
(northern works) New Road,
Whaley Bridge
High Peak
Derbyshire SK23 7JG
Tel: 01663 733544
(southern works)

Riverside Business Park
St Anne's Road
St Anne's Park
Bristol BS4 4ED
Tel: 01179 715337
www.dorothearestorations.
com

George James & Sons,
Blacksmiths
22 Cransley Hill
Broughton
Kettering
Northamptonshire
NN14 INB
Tel: 01536 790295

JH Porter & Son Ltd
13 Cranleigh Mews
Cabul Road
London SW11 2QL
Tel: 020 7978 5576
www.jhporter.co.uk

Kentish Ironcraft Ltd
Ashford Road
Bethersden, Ashford

Kent TN26 3AT
Tel: 01233 820465

JS Lunn and Sons
The Forge, Red Row
Morpeth, Northumberland
NE61 5AU
Tel: 01670 760246

Moulding & Panelling

Allied Guilds
Unit 19, Reddicap Trading
Estate, Coleshill Road
Sutton Coldfield
West Midlands B75 7BU
Te1: 01213 292874

Aristocast Originals
2 Wardsend Road
Sheffield S6 1RQ
Tel: 01142 344885
www.plasterware.net/
aristocast/

Butcher Plastering
Specialists Ltd
8 Fitzroy Road

Primrose Hill
London NW1 8TX
Tel: 020 7722 9771
www.butcherplasterworks.
com

Hallidays
Queen Street
Dorchester-on-Thames
Oxon OX10 7HL
Tel: 01865 340028
www.hallidays.com

Locker & Riley (Fibrous
Plastering) Ltd
Capital House
42–50 Bancrofts Road
South Woodham Ferrers
Chelmsford
Essex CM3 5UQ
Tel: 01245 322022
www.lockerandriley.com

Renaissance Mouldings Ltd
Unit 2, Abbey Mead
Industrial Park
Brooker Road

Waltham Abbey
Essex EN9 1HU
Tel: 01992 764666
www.renaissancemouldings.
com

John Powson
37 Thornton Street
Middlesbourough
Cleveland TS3 6PQ
Tel: 01642 211201

Stevensons of Norwich
Roundtree Way
Norwich NR7 8SQ
Tel: 01603 400824
www.stevensons-of-
norwich.co.uk

Winther Browne & Co Ltd
75 Bilton Way, Enfield
London EN3 7ER
Tel: 08456 121893
www.wintherbrowne.co.uk

Paints & Stains

Brodie & Middleton
68 Drury Lane
London WC2B 5SP
Tel: 020 7836 3289

Classic Finishes (Colourman
Paints)
140–146 Oak Street
Norwich NR3 3BP
Tel: 01603 760374
www.classicfinishes.co.uk

Cornelissen and Son Ltd
105 Great Russell Street
London WC1B 3RY
Tel: 020 7636 1045
www.cornelissen.com

Craig & Rose
Unit 8
Halbeath Industrial Estate
Dunfermline, Fife KY11 7EG
Tel: 0870 600 1829
www.craigandrose.com

Cy-pres (Brigstock) Ltd
14 Bells Close
Brigstock, Kettering
Northamptonshire NN14 3JG
Tel: 01536 373431

Dulux Heritage Range
ICI Paints
Wexham Road
Slough SL2 5DS
Tel: 08702 421100
www.heritagepaints.co.uk

Farrow & Ball Ltd
Uddens Industrial Estate
Wimbourne
Dorset BH21 7NL
Tel: 01202 876141
www.farrow-ball.com

Hirst Conservation
Materials Ltd
Laughton, Sleaford
Lincolnshire NG34 0HE
Tel: 01529 497517
www.hirst-conservation.
co.uk

John T Keep & Sons Ltd
PO Box 78
Croydon Road,
Elmers End
Beckenham, Kent
Tel: 020 8658 2299

Keim Mineral Paints Ltd
Muckley Cross
Morville, Nr Bridgnorth
Shropshire WV16 4RR
Tel: 01746 714543
www.keimpaints.co.uk

The Lime Centre
Long Barn, Morestead
Winchester
Hampshire SO21 1LZ
Tel: 01962 713636
www.thelimecentre.co.uk

Ludlow Period House Shop
141 Corve Street
Ludlow SY8 2PG
Tel: 01584 877276
www.periodhouseshops.com

John Oliver Ltd
33 Pembridge Road
London W11 3HG
Tel: 020 7221 6466
www.johnoliver.co.uk

Papers & Paints
4 Park Walk
London SW10 0AD
Tel: 020 7352 8626
www.papers-paints.co.uk

Potmolen Paint
27 Woodcock Industrial
Estate
Warminster
Wiltshire BA12 9DX
Tel: 01985 213960

Rose of Jericho
at St Blaise Ltd
Horchester Farm, Holywell
Nr. Evershot, Dorchester
Dorset DT2 0LL
Tel: 01935 83676
www.rose-of-jericho.demon.
co.uk

USA

Architectural Salvage Yards

Architectural Antiques
1321 East 2nd
Little Rock
Arkansas 72202
Tel: 501 372 1744

Architectural Salvage
Warehouse
337 Berry Street
Brooklyn, New York 11211
Tel: 718 388 4527

Irreplaceable Artifacts
428 Main Street
Middletown
Connecticut 06457
Tel: 860 344 8576
www.demolitiondepot.com

Jerard Paul Jordan Gallery
Slade Acres, PO Box 71
Ashford, Connecticut 06278
Tel: 204 429 7954

Joe Ley Antiques, Inc
615 East Market Street
Louisville
Kentucky 40202
Tel: 502 583 4014
www.joeley.com

Material Unlimited
2 West Michigan Avenue
Ypsilanti
Michigan 48197
Tel: 734 483 6980
www.materialsunlimited.com

Nostalgia Station
307 Stiles Avenue
Savannah. Georgia 31401
Tel: 912 232 8176

United House Wrecking
535 Hope Street
Stamford
Connecticut 06906-1300
Tel: 203 348 5371
www.unitedhousewrecking.com

Walker's
PO Box 309
Tallmadge, Ohio 44278
Tel: 330 633 1081

The Wrecking Bar
of Atlanta Inc
292 Moreland Avenue N.E.
Atlanta, Georgia 30307
Tel: 404 525 0468

Columns

Classic Architectural
Specialities
5302 Junius
Dallas, Texas 75214
Tel:214 827 3545

Dovetail
Box 1569
Lowell, Massachusetts
01853-2796
Tel: 800 344 5570

Haddonstone (USA) Ltd
201 Heller Place, Interstate
Business Park

Bellmawr, New Jersey 08031
Tel: 856 931 7011
www.haddonstone.com

Old South Columns
Moultrie Manufacturing
Company
PO Box 1179
Moultrie, Georgia 31768
Tel: 800 841 8674
www.moultriemanu
facturing.com

Robinson Iron
PO Box 1119
Alexander City. Alabama
35011-1119
Tel: 256 329 8486
www.robinsoniron.com

AF Schwerd
Manufacturing Co
3215 McClure Avenue
Pittsburgh
Pennsylvania 15212
Tel: 412 766 6322

Conservatories

Amdega Centre
160 Friendship Road
Cranbury, New Jersey 08512
Tel: 732 320 0999

Machin Design Builders
3 Hargrove Grade Suite 1
Palm Coast, Florida
Tel: 386 445 4350
www.machindesignbuilders.com

Oak Leaf Conservatories Ltd
876 Davis Drive
Atlanta, Georgia 30327
Tel: 800 360 6283
www.oakleafconservatories.com

Doors & Windows

Beech River Mill Company
30 Route 16B
Center Ossipee,
New Hampshire 03814
Tel: 603 539 2636
www.beechrivermill.com

Blaine Window
Hardware Inc
17319 Blaine Drive
Hagerstown
Maryland 21740
Tel: 301 797 6500
www.blainewindow.com

Historic Windows
PO Box 1172
Lakepointe
Harrisonburg
Virginia 22801
Tel: 540 434 5855

Hope's Windows Inc
84 Hopkins Ave
PO Box 580 Jamestown
New York 14702-0580
Tel: 716 655 5124
www.hopeswindows.com

Kenmore Industries Inc
146 Granite Street
Rockport
Massachusetts 1966
Tel: 978 546 6700

Marvin Windows
Warroad, Minnesota 56763
Tel: 218 386 1430
www.marvin.com

Materials Unlimited
2 West Michigan Avenue
Ypsilanti, Michigan 48197
Tel: 800 299 9462
www.materialsunlimited.com

Maurer & Shepherd
Joyners Inc
122 Naubuc Avenue
Glastonbury,
Connecticut 06033
Tel: 860 633 2383

Sheppard Millwork
21020 70th Avcnue West
Edmonds
Washington 98020
Tel: 425 771 4645

Silverton Victorian
Millworks
PO Box 2987

Durango, Colorado 81302
Tel: 800 933 3930

Walker's
PO Box 309
Tallmadge, Ohio 44278
Tel: 216 633 1081

The Woodstone Company
17 Morse Brook Road
Westminster
Vermont 05158
Tel: 802 722 9217
www.woodstone.com

Fabrics & Wallpapers
Laura Ashley
714 Madison Ave
New York, NY 10021
Tel: 212 735 5010

Brunschwig et Fils
979 Third Avenue
New York, NY 10022
Tel: 212 838 7878
www.brunschwig.com

SM Hexter Company
2800 Superior Avenue
Cleveland, Ohio 44114
Tel: 216 696 0146

Hodsoll McKenzie
Decoration & Design
Building, Suite 1616
979 Third Avenue
New York NY 10022
Tel: 212 759 5408

Lee Jofa
201 Central Avenue South
Bethpage, New York 11714
Tel: 800 453 3563
www.leejofa.com

Scalamandre
300 Trade Zone Drive
Ronkonkoma
New York 11779
Tel: 631 467 8800
www.scalamandre.com

F Schumacher & Co
The Decoration & Design

Building, Suite 611
979 Third Avenue
New York, NY 10022
Tel: 212 415 3900
www.fschumacher.com

Fireplaces & Stoves
Danny Alessandro Ltd
308 E 59th Street
New York, NY 10022
Tel: 212 421 1928
www.alessandroltd.com

Danny Alessandro Ltd
8409 Santa Monica
Boulevard
Los Angeles
California 90069
Tel: 213 654 6198
www.alessandroltd.com

Barnstable Stove Shop
PO Box 472
West Barnstaple
Massachusetts 02668
Tel: 508 362 9913
www.barnstablestove.com

Bryant Stove &
Music Inc
27 Stovepipe Alley,
Thorndike, Maine 04986
Tel: 207 568 3665
www.bryantstove.com

Driwood Molding Company
PO Box 1729
Florence
South Carolina 29503
Tel: 843 669 2478
www.driwood.com

CG Girolami & Co
944 N Spaulding Ave
Chicago, Illinois 60651
Tel: 773 227 1959

Nostalgia Station
307 Stiles Avenue
Savannah, Georgia 31401
Tel: 912 232 8176

Vermont Structural
Slate Co Ltd
Box 98, 3 Prospect Street
Fair Haven, Vermont 05743
Tel: 802 265 4933
www.vermontstructuralslate.
com

Hardware

Anglo Amcrican Brass Co
PO Box 9487
San José, California 95157
Tel: 408 246 0203

The Village Smithy
26 South Third Street
Wolcott, Vermont 05680
Tel: 970 963 9990

Tremont Nail Company
PO Box 31
Mansfield,
Massachusetts 02048
Tel: 800 835 0121
www.tremontnail.com

Williamsburg Blacksmiths
26 Williams Street
Williamsburg,
Massachusetts 01096
Tel: 800 248 1776
www.williamsburgblacksmiths.
com

The Woodbury Blacksmith
and Forge Co
125 Main Street
PO Box 268
Woodbury, Connecticut
06798
Tel: 203 263 5737

Kitchens

Alno Ltd
4232 El Camino Real
Palo Alto, California 94306
Tel: 650 843 0754
www.europeankitchendesign.
com

Poggenpohl USA Corp
350 Passaic Avenue
Fairfield, New Jersey 07004
Tel: 973 812 8900
www.poggenpohl-usa.com

Siematic of Los Angeles
8687 Melrose Avenue
West Hollywood
California 90069
Tel: 310 659 6147

Smallbone Inc
135 E 65th Street
New York, NY 10022
Tel: 212 288 3454
www.smallboneofdevizes.
com

Lighting

Authentic Designs
The Mill Road
West Rupert
Vermont 05776
Tel: 800 844 9416
www.authenticdesigns.com

B&P Lamp Supply Inc
843 Old Morrison Highway,
McMinnville
Tennessee 37110
Tel: 931 473 3016
www.bplampsupply.com

Ball and Ball
463 W Lincoln Highway
Exton
Pennsylvania 19341-2705
Tel: 800 257 3711
www.ballandball-us.com

City Lights
2226 Massachusetts Ave
Cambridge. MA 02140
Tel: 617 547 1490

Colonial Metalcrafters
The Brass Lion
5935 S. Broadway
Tyler, Texas 75701
Tel: 903 561 1111

AJP Coppersmith & Co
34 Broadway Street
Wakefield, Maine 01880
Tel: 781 245 1216
www.ajpcoppersmith.com

Hurley Patentee Manor
464 Old Route 209
Hurley, New York 12443

Tel: 845 331 5414
www.hurleypatenteelighting.
com

King's Chandelier Co
Dept 1, PO Box 667
Eden
North Carolina 27289
Tel: 336 623 6188
www.chandelier.com

Lamplight
302 West Maple Street
Nicholasville
Kentucky 40356
Tel: 859 533 3293

The London Venturers Co
2 Dock Square
Rockport
Massachusetts 01966
Tel: 978 546 7161

Gates Moore
Water Street
South Norwalk
Connecticut 06850

Tel: 203 847 3231
www.gatesmoore
lighting.com

Paxton Hardware Ltd
PO Box 256
Upper Falls
Maryland 21156
Tel: 800 241 9741
www.paxtonhardware.com

Progress Lighting
119 Rockland Center 305
Nanuet
New York 10954-2964
Tel: 888 844 3332
www.progresslighting.com

Rejuvenation House Parts
2550 NW Nicolai Street
Portland, Oregon 97210
Tel: 888 401 1900
www.rejuvenation.com

Renovation Concepts
9550 SW Beaverton
Hillsdale Highway

Beaverton
Oregon 97005
Tel: 503 619 4663
www.renovationconcepts.net

Roy Electric Co
22 Elm Street
Westfield New Jersey 7090
Tel: 800 366 3347
www.royelectric.com

The Saltbox
3004 Columbia Avenue
Lancaster, Pennsylvania
17603
Tel: 717 392 5649

St Louis Antique
Lighting Co
801 N Skinker Blvd
St Louis, Missouri 63130
Tel: 314 863 1414

Shaker Workshops
PO Box 8001
Ashburnham
Massachusetts 01430-8001

Tel: 800 840 9121
www.shakerworkshops.com

Stair & Co Ltd
942 Madison Avenue
New York, NY 10021
Tel: 212 517 4400

Sturbridge Yankee
Workshop
Portland, Maine
Tel: 800 231 8060
www.sturbridgeyankee.com

Metalwork & Fencing

Architectural Iron Company
104 Ironwood Court
Box 126
Milford
Pennsylvania 18337-0126
Tel: 570 296 7722
www.architecturaliron.com

Cassidy Bros Forge Inc
US Route I
Rowley,
Massachusetts 01969

Tel: 978 948 7303
www.cassidybros.com

Moultrie Manufacturing
Company
PO Box 1179
Moultrie, Georgia 31768
Tel: 800 841 8674
www.moultriemanufacturing.
com

Nostalgia Station
307 Stiles Avenue
Savannah.
Georgia 31401
Tel: 912 232 8176

Robinson Iron
PO Box 1119
Alexander City,
Alabama 35011-1119
Tel: 256 329 8486
www.robinsoniron.com

Stewart Manufacturing Co
PO Box 2612
Covington,

Kentucky 41012-0001
Tel: 859 431 1985

Walpole Woodworkers
767 East Street
Walpole,
Massachusetts 02081
Tel: 508 668 2800
www.walpolewoodworkers.
com

Moulding & Panelling

Bendix Moldings
465 South Dean Street
Englewood
New Jersey 07631
Tel: 201 567 1003
www.bendixarchitectural.
com

Classic Architectural
Specialities
5302 Junius
Dallas, Texas 75214
Tel: 214 827 3545

Cumberland Woodcraft
Co Inc
PO Drawer 609
Carlisle
Pennsylvania 17013-0609
Tel: 717 243 0063
www.cumberlandwoodcraft.
com

Dovetail
Box 1569
Lowell
Massachusetts 01853-2796
Tel: 800 344 5570

Driwood Molding Company
PO Box 1729
Florence
South Carolina 29503
Tel: 843 669 2478
www.driwood.com

CG Girolami & Co
944 N Spaulding Ave
Chicago, Illinois 60651
Tel: 773 227 1959

Gold Leaf Conservation
Studios
The Gratz Gallery
30 West Bridge Street
PO Box 118
New Hope, Pennsylvania
18938
Tel: 215 862 4300
www.gratzgallery.com

Haas Wood &
Ivory Works Inc
184A Harbor Road
San Francisco,
California 94124-2470
Tel: 650 588 1082

Mark A. Knudsen
1100 East County Line Road
Des Moines
Iowa 50320
Tel: 515 285 6112

Mad River Woodworks
PO Box 1067
Blue Lake
California 95525-1067

Tel: 707 668 5671
www.madriverwoodworks

Maurer & Shepherd
Joyners Inc
122 Naubuc Avenue
Glastonbury
Connecticut 06033
Tel: 860 633 2383

Mendocino Millwork
Hallelujah Redwood
Products
PO Box 669
Mendocino
California 95460-0669
Tel: 707 937 4410

W.F Norman Corporation
PO Box 323
214 N Cedar Street
Nevada, Missouri 64772
Tel: 800 641 4038
www.wfnorman.com

Nostalgia Station
307 Stiles Avenue

Savannah, Georgia 31401
Tel: 912 232 8176

Royal American
Wallcraft, Inc
501 Central Avenue
Crescent City
Florida 33450
Tel: 800 330 9435
www.countnine.com/rawi/

Sheppard Millwork
21020 70th Avenue West
Edmonds
Washington 98020
Tel: 425 771 4645

Silverton Mill Works
Box 850-FAA
Silverton
Colorado 81433
Tel: 303 387 5716

WP Stephens Lumber Co
145 Church Street
Marietta, Georgia 30061
Tel: 404 428 1531

Tiresias Inc
PO Box 1864
Orangeburg,
South Carolina
29116 1864
Tel: 803 534 8478

Vintage Wood Works
513 S Adams Dept 704
Fredericksburg, Texas 78624
Tel: 512 997 9513

Walker's
PO Box 309
Tallmadge, Ohio 44278
Tel: 330 633 1081

JP Weaver Company
941 Air Way
Glendale, California 91201
Tel: 818 500 1798
www.jpweaver.com

Paints & Stains
Evergreene Painting
Studios Inc
450 West 31st Street

New York, NY 10001-4608
Tel: 212 244 2800
www.evergreene.com

Gold Leaf
Conservation Studios
The Gratz Gallery
30 West Bridge Street
PO Box 118
New Hope
Pennsylvania 18938
Tel: 215 862 4300
www.gratzgallery.com

Martin Senour Company
Tel: 800 526 6704
www.martinsenour.com

Benjamin Moore & Co
101 Paragon Drive
Montvale, NJ 07645
www.benjaminmoore.com

The Old Fashioned Milk
Paint Company
436, Main Street
Groton

Massachusetts 01450
Tel: 866 350 6455
www.milkpaint.com

Pratt & Lambert
www.prattandlambert.com

Rust Construction Co
210 S Payne Street
Alexandria, Vermont 22314
Tel: 703 836 6010

Index